What others are saying about Freetown Christiania:

Hi Eugine,
I have just finished your book.
It was brilliant. Interesting reading indeed.
Gay Leverington

I love the book Eugine, thanks for sharing a part of life with us. I was hooked from the start and just couldn't put it down until I finished. When is your next one coming out???????
Chris Sheldrick

Hey Eugine, Awesome book. Engaging, descriptive - couldn't put it down. Thanks for sharing your story, will look out for any more books that you put out.
Emma Boyle-Shaw

This is a classic read.....good insight into anarchy as an option! Surprisingly engaging....I'm looking forward to any follow up reading on this society, if we can call it that!
Sean Clifford

Eugine Losse

Freetown Christiania

Copyright © 2011 Ben Ashman

All rights reserved.

ISBN:14664946754
ISBN-13:978-1466496750

For Karen.

ON THE ROAD

Squatting on the side of the freeway leaning forward onto my backpack, hugging it with my arms, squeezing it between my thighs, eyes closed, resting. Standing all day on the bitumen thumbing rides has left me exhausted. Today, yesterday, the day before and I've only managed three or four hundred kilometres out of Stockholm.

    A truck roars past and I feel the vibrating road through my jaw resting on the backpack, which gets caught in the slipstream and lolls my body from side to side as I squat like a junky craving a fix of distance, a gram of movement, just a little bit of motion to see me through. I listen for the slowing of engine revolutions, the squealing of breaks, anything that indicates a car is stopping, but nothing, just the regular humming of freeway traffic. Standing up, opening my eyes, a fork in the freeway stretches out before me, a long, fast exit from the highway onto a smaller, alternate route. It has been hours since I was dropped at this nowhere spot, the rain has come and gone and an icy wind blows down from the Arctic. My thumb juts out through a hole in a sock, extended high for drivers to see. Sooner or later someone will stop.

    Closing my eyes, feeling the cars swoosh by, wondering what Carmen is doing. Last I knew she was headed to Scotland, but talking about going to South America, I wonder if she made it. My lovely Carmen, with a voice so rich that when she sings people still themselves and listen, focusing on the beautiful sounds that float from her soul, all else forgotten. Flowing red hair, high cheekbones, thousands of freckles, she was willing to sleep under the stars and go where the cars took us, but I felt the need to travel alone, unhindered, free.

    The squealing of old brakes! I open my eyes as an ancient, decrepit Volvo scrunches the gravel on the freeway's shoulder and stops. It has a long, twisted gash in the passenger door which is framed with red rust and its pistons clang loudly as though they are ricocheting straight off of bare metal. The driver is a little younger than thirty with long, wavy hair, pulled loosely into a pony tail. He's wearing only a singlet, despite the cold, the heater blasting hot air through the car.

The driver talks about his travels in India, describing the Himalayas and how he walked for months on end carrying only a small bag containing a change of clothes and a silk sleeping bag. We talk and talk as the countryside slips by until he drops me at an intersection to a road that leads to his grandmother's house.

The Volvo clunks off down the road coughing a bluish haze from its half hanging off exhaust pipe. The clanging of its pistons slowly fades into the distance. A slight drizzle dampens my clothes, but I enjoy the isolation not caring that the few cars that drive past do not stop. After a while I don't even bother to lift my arm or extend my thumb, caring only to kick stones across the freeway and smoke roll-ups, wondering if there are any wild deer roaming in the forest beyond the chain link fence.

An old lady stops and drives me a short distance to a truck stop. The sun slowly slips. Not quite a sunset, but rather the beginning of a long Scandinavian dusk with an orange glow that persists for hours across the sky. I'm freeway surfing, paddling with a thumb, anticipating the next wave, floating way out back of life's gentle, rolling swell, peeking down the road waiting for the next wave to arrive. And it does, rising steeply out of the bitumen in the form of a dirty big truck, hissing air and belching fumes. The driver speaks little English so I have no idea where he is heading, but as long as it is forwards I don't care. Distance has found me as the wave surges forward hauling all the steel in the world. The driver grins like a jester. It's all smiles, steel, the road and a soft voice crooning from the radio in the truck's massive dashboard as my body relaxes into the movement through another fix of distance.

Little more than an hour later we reach the docks at Holsenborg in the far south of Sweden. It has just gone midnight and I'm hoping that my wave doesn't break just yet, but it does. The driver indicates I must leave the cab before his truck boards the ferry, something to do with the law. An icy sea wind blows over the exposed docks and I quickly have socks on my hands and my hat pulled down tightly on my head. A midnight worker tells me that the next ferry is due to leave in a few minutes so I strain my heart dashing to its point of departure, paddling like crazy to catch the next wave. I encounter a guard on the gangway wanting to check my ticket, which I do not possess, and I've no Swedish currency having spent my last on a stick of salami two days ago. The guard takes pity and allows me to pass regardless. My wave surges forward and I am surfing once again.

The ferry journey from Sweden across to Denmark will only take twenty minutes, so I find a row of seats and occupy them all by stretching out and resting against my bag. My hair is knotted and my clothes unwashed, holes in the toes of my shoes and an unshaven face, quite a contrast to the well groomed tourists pacing the decks and browsing the gift shops. It's late, well past midnight when a tall skinny man comes along. He's staggering and finding it difficult to stay upright atop the gentle sway of the moving ferry. Dressed in denim he has a half-grown beard, shaggy hair and a stuffed duck, the type won in fairground sideshows, tucked under an arm. With his free hand he points to my hat and slurs something in Swedish.

"Sorry bud, don't speak Swedish," I say.

"Oh, you don't speak Swedish? Well, lucky I speak English," he says. "I said: great hat."

"Thanks, a friend gave it to me."

He wobbles, holding his duck as though it aids him in the struggle to remain upright. He stinks of beer.

"It's the colour of my football team. Where're you going?" His bloodshot eyes have locked onto my bags.

"South."

"Want a lift?" he slurs, looking back to me.

"Not with you, man, you're drunk!"

"No, no, no," he says waving his hand about to dismiss my concerns. "My friend, he's driving." He staggers, as the ferry takes a sudden lurch. "Come on."

I follow Duckman.

When I see his cohorts I curse the lead that I've followed. There are three of them, hooting around a table piled high with empty beer cans and an overflowing ashtray. All appear drunk and I wonder which of them is driving, the lanky guy with moustache and psychotic eyes, or the young guy in a leather jacket? The young guy is laughing, a hysterical laugh. I would not trust him behind the wheel of a car. Duckman tells me it's the tall lanky guy who is driving, the psychotic who does not speak. A voice booms over the ferry's public announcement system, first in Swedish, then Danish, German, and finally English, requesting passengers to prepare to disembark. I follow their staggering lead downstairs and into the ferry's car park.

We sit like racers on the grid in the belly of the ferry. A hundred cars revving engines while waiting until the huge doors to swing open. Our ride races out into the late night, accelerating through the stampede until the swirling freshness of the ocean's air is gone and we find ourselves deep in the country. Dance beats crank through the stereo loud enough to have to shout to be heard. "So, where're you all off to?" I yell to the young guy in the leather jacket squashed next to me in the back seat.

"Don't know," he shrugs. "I met these guys in a bar earlier and they kidnapped me."

"They kidnapped you?" I shout back.

"Yeah, well, you see it was my grandmother's eighty-fourth birthday today and this morning I went to her place for a big family lunch. One of my cousins had some acid so we dropped it and the next thing I knew it was dark and I was in a bar in the city, without my cousin, dancing to crappy old disco music. I accidently spilt a drink on the guy with the duck; does he actually have a duck?"

"Yeah he does."

"Oh, great, I though the acid was still playing with me. Is it dead? How come it's so still?"

"It's stuffed."

"Shit, I've been thinking it was real, man that doesn't make any sense. Anyway, I spilt a drink on him and the next thing I know I'm being pushed into the back seat of this car."

"You don't know these guys?"

"No idea, they scared the shit out of me at first, but they're okay, just having fun I guess. My mum is going to be pissed at me for missing my grandmother's birthday; did I tell you she's turning eighty-four today? My mum's going to be so angry when she finds out I'm in Norway."

"We're not in Norway."

"What?"

"Denmark, we're in Denmark. I think we're headed towards Copenhagen."

"Oh, shit, hey have you seen my shoe, I think I've lost one?"

I look down to his feet, "You haven't lost a shoe."

"I've lost something. I thought it was my shoe?"

Duckman, sitting in the front passenger seat, turns and yells: "Want a beer?"

"Sure!" Of course, may as well join them.

The night streams its blackness through the open windows and I can feel the power of my wave surging forwards carrying me on to my future destination. There is a sign on the freeway pointing south and it is not indicating the direction that we are travelling.

"Hey," I yell to the driver. "Drop me off before Copenhagen, I'm heading south. I don't want to go to the city." Psycho looks at me in the rear vision mirror. He doesn't blink.

"Where you going?" asks Kidnap

"South," I yell as a hash-pipe is passed across to me. "It's too frigging cold up here!"

Giant blocks of ugly concrete, apartments, cascade past the car's window. "Hey," I yell above the music to the driver. "Hey buddy, stop the car, let me out. I'm not going to Copenhagen. South, man, I'm going south. It's too damn cold up here!" He doesn't respond, not even a blink.

"We've kidnapped you!" yells Duckman and laughs manically.

Kidnap enters into fits of laughter and passes me another beer. A nice bed in the country grass it might have been, but I can't exit my wave as it carries me straight onto the rocks of the largest city in northern Europe. Grey apartment blocks, five stories high; traffic lights, the swoosh of cars. The lights and sounds, the smells, there's no escaping the city. It has swallowed me once again.

After circling Copenhagen's inner city, Psycho finally parks the car and immediately the police are accosting us. I waver on the curb, not understanding the argument between the Swedes and the police. Duckman is pointing his finger at a policeman seeming to believe that he's controlling the situation. The duck slips from under his arm and he staggers while bending to retrieve it. The police leave, appearing to not want the hassle associated with drunken foreigners. A neon sign periodically colours itself red, Maxim's Bar, we go in.

Opposite the bar dim lights glow red behind booth seats. The room is long, but narrow. At the far end is a raised dance floor lined with mirrors on which a topless girl slowly dances, barely managing to hide her boredom. A couple of men idle away their midnight hours perversely contemplating their bank balances and sipping overpriced spirits. Two of the men, a little older than the rest, must have money as a large group of girls flutter seductively around them. Duckman and Psycho make their way to the far end of the room towards a man sitting alone in a booth. They speak briefly then disappear through a hidden door.

Some of the girls smell new blood in the bar. "Buy me drink, buy me drink! How much money you have?" they're blunt and not in the least attractive despite their pretty faces and taut bodies.

"None." I don't need to lie.

"You lie. How much money you have?"

"None." She drifts away pouting contempt.

A second girl grasps her opportunity and sits close, her breath stinks of salt. "Where're you from? What're you doing here?" She's getting closer, shooting questions as a distraction. I can feel her hand brushing over my thigh feeling for a wallet that does not exist.

The dancing girls change, all as uninterested as the first. They take turns coaxing drinks, all very determined. Duckman and Psycho return from the back room, not looking happy. "We're leaving. The girls are too expensive here, we'll find somewhere else."

They walk out leaving Kidnap and me on a warm, spongy sofa. "This place is shit," says Kidnap. "I'm going to buy some hash, you coming?"

"We got something better than hash," whispers a girl in my ear. "We got something much better." She places her finger to her nose and sniffs. Her eyes don't coordinate.

"Yeah, sure I'll come." I smile at Kidnap and swing my bag up onto my shoulder.

Up on the street with the wind blown trash and junkies hunched over in the gutter a cab is hailed. It races away, me and Kidnap in the back seat, keen to escape the city's filth. The taxi turns a couple of tight corners then squeezes through an even tighter laneway before crossing a bridge over a wide canal and finally halting beside a dirt path leading into tree shrouded darkness. It is odd seeing so many trees down this dirt laneway in the middle of a city street. Kidnap pays the fare and I see on the dashboard that it has just gone three in the morning. This part of the city is asleep and the street is quiet. Old three and four-story apartment buildings in various stages of dilapidation stretch up and down the street, while a beautiful church with a spiral staircase winding its way around a tall steeple stands before us. Just across the road a vacant lot is covered in bitumen and cordoned off by a concrete wall and wire mesh fencing. Except for the magnificence of the steeple it is a pretty normal scene for most any city. Normal, that is except for this dirt path that meanders off past lush, wild trees and into pitch darkness. The path appears out of place within the city, as though it belongs in the countryside. A sign supported by thick poles spans the path on which large, irregular letters announce, Christiania.

My vision reaches little more than twenty metres beyond the sign where the dirt path widens and is swallowed by the dark. To the left is a large, three-story barn-like building constructed with aged wooden planks, out of place in the city. To the right is a wall covered with a big colourful mosaic made from irregular shaped tiles. The path takes a slight turn to the left and reveals a tiny light in the distance where it widens to become a dirt street lined with weary old buildings, three stories high on the left, one story high on the right.

Morning is only a couple of hours away and the street is almost deserted. We pass a bakery and a man shuffles away from its counter and out of sight. The air has become very cold, but my leather keeps me warm. Kidnap bangs his hands together as he walks. The light comes from a hut where two men are talking. One alters his posture acknowledging our approach. His hair is thick, falling straight down to his shoulders. A grubby parka defends his warmth and a black beret is pulled down tight to his ears, a Greenlander, a businessman. He's working and his interest in us is nothing less than professional. Huge chunks of hash lay on a card table before him. Kidnap begins to haggle, mixing the gruff tones of Danish with the melodies of the Swedish language. He's lifting the blocks to his nose and smelling the hash, comparing them to one another and offering prices. The Greenlander shakes his head refusing. Kidnap pauses for a second then nods before passing a flurry of Danish notes to the Greenlander, who bites off a piece of hash, clips it to a small spring scale dangled from his fingers and weighs it: 2.5 grams. He gives it to Kidnap.

Over the road and further into the village a large wooden shack shines a light through its windows. Woodstocks is written across its worn timbers, standing out against a painted background of flowers and trees. A shambling veranda leads around to a door where a couple of drunks slouch against the splitting timbers and grumble at us as we enter a room brimming with argument. Spittle arcs through the stale, smoky air as people jab fingers at one another and slosh beer across the floor. A montage of contorted, red faces display the anger, insult, disgust and revenge of the patrons. They stagger about from one argument to the next interjecting and shouting in an orgy of disagreement and I can only assume that these people, this Woodstock's crowd, are very familiar with each other. The arguing that Kidnap and I have walked into is not among strangers but those who know each other well, like an extended family at a Christmas dinner, or rather, five or six hours of heavy drinking following a Christmas dinner. They are so ferocious in their shouting and finger pointing that I fear that blows will be struck, but are not. Faces turn red, fists are waved, but there is no violence. In fact, the more I watch the fracas the more I tend to think that the arguing is actually the manner in which these people entertain themselves. Underneath the hostility they seem to be enjoying themselves.

Kidnap buys a couple of beers and we exit the bar to drink on the veranda and watch the drunks outside. They scream and shout at each other like little children fighting over a toy, but with gruff voices and stunted movements. Another drunk staggers from the bar to piss on a bush. A woman follows him out and squats, pulling her pants down around her ankles. She continues to argue, tossing her arms around in the air, as she ejects a hot stream of piss.

Kidnap drops a block of hash on a worn wooden table and torches it with a flame from a lighter. He picks up the block as it smoulders with a wisp of smoke and crumbles it over a large cigarette paper. He rolls a tight cylinder with a torn piece of cardboard and places it at one end of the paper. Tobacco is added and the mixture is firmly rolled together before he runs his tongue across the glue and finally produces a joint. Holding it high he lights the excess paper and it flickers into life. He passes it to me.

The temperature has dropped very low and condensation catches our breath. Not far away a fire burns in a steel drum and people are warming their hands by it. The promise of warmth urges us to join the two men and a woman with their arms stretched over the flames. They listen to a tall, slender, angular man dressed in black who stands across the fire. My hands enjoy the flame.

The man speaks a monologue in Danish, the foreign language a perfect wash of ambience over the fire's flicking flames. After some time he turns to me. "So you speak English then, eh?"

"Yeah."

The fire's company switches its attention towards me as he continues, "I see you have a bag. You've just arrived, yes?"

"Only an hour ago." I answer.

"This late in the night? Are you running from something?"

"Running?" I ask.

"Yeah, many people are running from something, sometimes they come to Christiania to escape."

"Nah, I'm not really running. Except from the cold weather I guess. I just want to stay away from cities, although here I find myself in another one."

He appears offended. "What, Christiania? This is not a city, man."

"Yeah, Copenhagen," and I point down towards the gates of Christiania and to the city beyond.

"No, man, Copenhagen may as well be a million miles away. Christiania is not Copenhagen. It is separate. Copenhagen ends as soon as you walk under that gate. He holds his hands wide apart for emphasis.

"How, what do you mean?"

"Well, the law for one, the law that Danish people live under, just over there," He too indicates the street just beyond Christiania's entrance. "It doesn't apply here. Christiania is a free town, man. No law, no police, no government, no city."

"What, anarchy?" I question.

"Anarchy, whatever, but yeah, if that's the way you want to describe it. I guess, yes, anarchy."

"Is it violent?" I ask. My father always used the word anarchy whenever he saw something on the news about civil wars in some far off country. He talked about anarchy as it was the most violent and terrible state of human existence.

"Violent!" laughs the man. "No, man, violence is for the straight world, governments are violent, police are violent, laws are violent. Christiania, we're not violent, anything but violent. In fact if you were violent here in Christiania you would find yourself marched out before you could even put your bags down. Anarchy is the rejection of violence, man. Violence as a form of control is the exact opposite of anarchy. Out there in the city is the violence. Those straight people need violence to maintain their fucking straight world. The truth is they are controlled by violence."

"No," I say, yet interested.

"Well, out there in the straight world, let's say you don't pay your taxes, or you don't register your car to drive on the roads. What happens?" It's a rhetorical question and he doesn't wait for me to answer. "The law says you are wrong, a criminal. The police come and tell you that you must go to court, you go to court and you get a fine and you decide not to pay the fine, what happens then?" Once again the question is rhetorical and he continues after only a short pause. "Well, then the police come again and say that you have to go to jail, but you don't want to go so they grab you and try to handcuff you and you resist. Then they use even more force and before you know it you have two cops clamping your hands behind your back and slamming you in jail. This is violence, governments control people by violence. They legitimise themselves by their willingness to use violence. If you play by the rules and obey the law you are personally spared their violence. If you don't, they believe that they have the right, the authority to commit violence against you. Even if you do play by their rules governments believe that they have the right to use violence against others in your name. Democracies are not benevolent my friend, they are institutions that think they have the authority to use violence against those who disagree."

"Yeah, but you have to pay your taxes, don't you?" Not that I really believe in paying my taxes.

"Why? I mean, I was born in Denmark, but I didn't choose to be. Just because I am born here why I am then obligated to financially support the government? Why do I have to pay my taxes so the police can be paid to come and lock me up if I smoke a joint? Why do I have to pay my taxes so the government can drop a bomb on some poor schoolhouse on the other side of the world because it wants their oil? I don't believe, and most people in Christiania don't believe that we are obligated to pay for a government that exists because of the violence that it is willing to perpetrate against its citizens and other countries. Why should I accept the government's authority to commit violence against its people and innocents on the other side of the world? No way, anarchy isn't violent; it is the rejection of violence. Anyway, in Christiania we are a free town and life is different from out in the city. We have no laws to govern us or police to stop crime. When we see someone unknown, a stranger, arrive with bags in the middle of the night we take notice of them. So when I ask you if you are running from something it isn't out of curiosity. Be sure that Christiania will be watching you."

"Yeah, well I wasn't planning on staying. I never knew Christiania existed until tonight. I'm heading south anyway."

"Hey man," he says. "Like Bob Dylan says, to live outside the law you have to be honest."

With this he seems content and becomes silent, arms outstretched over the fire. One of the company gives me a look, as if to say, "Whatever, the guy's crazy."

The fire is in a gravel square ten metres on each side. On the closest side is another bar, it's closed. Grass grows across the roof of the bar and its sign reads: Nemoland. To the right is a small children's playground enclosed by a chest-high wooden plank fence. Next to it is a theatre stage, five metres across with a half dome above it. I bid farewell to the fire's company and heft my bag towards the stage. Kidnap remains by the fire warming his hands.

The stage is waist high. Wiping my finger across its surface I make a clean line in the dust. Already filthy I throw my kit up onto the stage and climb after. My night time falls and I sleep.

A CRAZY LITTLE VILLAGE

The morning sun wakes me, but fails to save my bones from the dawn's chill. In the early hours of the morning an old bum has also crashed on the stage. His face is gruff and covered chin to lip with a matted, unkempt beard. He too is stirring. His slight frame sits up, head lolling as if it is too heavy for his narrow neck and shoulders. A second bum arrives at the stage. This one is shorter and healthier with feathers and beads twisted into his beard. They smoke hash from a chillum. It's such a fine day and already the sky is clearing to a hollow blue, a hopeful sign that the day's warmth is not far away. There is no sign of Kidnap anywhere and I smile as I picture him trying to get back across the water to Sweden after the most bizarre eighty fourth birthday he will probably ever attend.

I have no water so my first action for the day is decided. Scouting around the stage I can't find a tap and am forced to venture further. Gathering my bag I bid farewell to the bums and make way along a path to find a dull concrete building, two stories high. A bearded old man sits on a bench by the door lending his attention to the intricacies of carving wood. I request water and he directs me through the door. "Turn right and there you'll find a bathroom…the water is in the tap." From beneath his slouch he peers up at me through shiny glasses, smiling with kindness in his eyes.

Having fished a bread-roll, cheese and salami from my bag I return to the gravel square to sit on a bench preparing food. The healthier of the bums I met earlier spies me and sits close by to talk. "This place, Christiania, is run by the Hell's Angels," he says proudly. His tanned and wrinkled face twitches and contorts, making his matted beard dance around on his face like a small, wild animal. "And I am one of them. Here see my badge."

He extracts a shiny silver medallion from a pocket in his leather jacket. Hells Angels is engraved across its surface with a serial number written underneath. "A while ago, Christiania was run by Bullshit."

My face contorts to a question mark. The Angel explains, "Bullshit are, were," he adds with a smile, "a biker gang, like the Hells Angels, only not so tough. A while ago there was a war going over the drug trade in Christiania, speed, smack, coke, that sort of thing. Half the junk in Europe once came out of this place. You see Christiania's like a fortress, a place where the police can't come, but now there's no junk, none at all, Christiania has gone clean." His brow deepens while he thinks for a moment before adding, "Thank those bloody mothers for that."

"What's that about mothers?" I ask, thinking they are another biker gang, but he's already back on track.

"Back then when the junk was coming and going the Angels kicked some ass man. Some brothers were killed, but Bullshit went down. You see that bar, Nemoland?" He points with a yellow stained finger.

I nod.

"The leader of Bullshit is buried under the concrete foundations of that bar. The war ended when the Hells Angels killed him. Now Bullshit is gone and Christiania is to the Hell's Angels." The Angel speaks with obvious pride. "I'm old now, but still I'm an Angel!"

"I see." I am nervous not to offend him, yet curious that he has no insignia on his jacket. "You don't wear the Hells Angel patch?" I question him, brave before an old bum. It has been bothering me ever since he showed his membership badge that he seems to prize so much.

The Angel glares at me angrily. As he hesitates the air thickens between us, "Those bloody women!" He storms off a frustrated old man.

Nemoland is opening. A large, bearded man sweeps the outside area of the bar. Another giant of a man with booming muscles wheels a barrow laden with tools through the gravel square. Tattoos swirl around his arms disappearing under his T-shirt to emerge up the back of his neck: skulls and daggers, naked women and demons, a biker for sure. He halts at the edge of Nemoland to unload the barrow and I'm thinking he is another Hell's Angel, but he doesn't display the Angel patch either.

Life is teetering around. Mothers with prams and dogs of all sizes meander through the gravel square. I see that they're not called Great Danes without reason as they appear more like horses than dogs. A couple of dreadlocked, tea cozzied, Rastafarians sit on a log by a sign that reads: Grøntsagen. A blonde lady walks out a nearby door carrying a brown paper bag overflowing with fruit, waving to a friend. Children chase after each other on old rickety bikes and a couple of bums lean against a tree sipping at their wine.

Journeying south is still on my mind, but the day is becoming quite warm and I have developed a fascination for this strange village in the middle of a city. My bag, even though it's not large or heavy, is a burden to lug around. I need to find a place to stash it and remember the kindness of the old man carving wood who gave me water.

Still on his bench he is now among company. A ragged but happy looking bunch of middle aged men all supping from beers as the sun grows strong and bright. The new faces eye me cautiously, but the old man acknowledges my return with a slight smile, moving his carving knife to the bench beside him. His smile lends me courage to speak among the group of strangers. "I'm wondering if I could leave my bag in the building while I look around the village?" I ask as if I'm a little boy requesting a cookie from my grandmother.

"You want to leave your bags here, with us?" He repeats my question as though it has surprised him.

"Is it a problem?" I say. "Because if it is…"

"Noooo, no it's no problem," he widens his smile. "You're Australian, yes?"

"Yes," I reply, surprised that he can guess my origins so easily from my accent.

"Then of course you can leave your kit. It's funny," he chuckles. "I knew that the day would come that I'd have to repay an Aussie. I've been waiting a long while, but I always knew it'd come."

"Sorry?" I haven't a clue what he's talking about.

"No matter, you see through the door to those stairs?" He turns and points through the door of the drab concrete building to the base of a set of thick wooden stairs. "You can leave your kit under the stairs, but be sure to take your money. I'm not responsible."

One of the guys standing around spits out a swig of beer. "No, Neils is not responsible."

Neils looks at the guy sharply, but I can tell it's in fun.

"I am only repeating the Judge, they're his words!" The guy defends himself from Neil's glare.

I drag my bag towards the building and above its door I notice a sign. It reads: W.C. FIELDS. The letters are carved into the wood and I guess it to be a clubhouse sign. Inside a musty smell affronts my nostrils.

Immediately to the left of the door is a table with six chairs. A couple of feet further in is a table tennis table and beyond that a huge kitchen with dirty dishes piled high. To the right is a snooker table and a game of table soccer. The floor is nothing more than a concrete slab so the place is cool and has a warehouse feeling about it. Despite all its contents there is plenty of room as each wall is no less than six metres long. A set of stairs leads up to a loft that takes up about a quarter of the total ceiling space. I hide my bags under the stairs.

The group of men are laughing and yelling at each other in Danish as I walk back out of the W.C. Fields Clubhouse. "Thank you, I won't be long," I say to Neils when I catch his eye.

"Hey Aussie, you need a place to stay?" says Neils, more a statement than a question.

"Well," I reply unsure of how to answer. "I might be leaving,"

"Ha!" he rises and places a hand on my shoulder. "I owe you as much as a place to sleep."

"Why?" It unnerves me that he feels he owes me something.

"Do I need a reason to help a fellow traveller? But I do have one, karma. Up in that loft, you can sleep tonight. If you want to that is."

"Okay, thanks!" I say, then set off towards the gravel square. "See you later."

"That you will," he replies then sips at a beer and continues his wood carving.

A path leads up onto the roof of Nemoland where grass grows thick and lush, then follows a ridge away from the square and sweeps down to the banks of a lake, in the middle of which is a small overgrown island. Beyond the opposite shoreline Copenhagen looms. Buildings peer over a high wall like children sneaking a look into a forbidden garden. They are deleted as the path enters a canopy of foliage so thick it hides the sky. Roots from tough old trees sprout from the ground reclaiming the earth from the cracked bitumen that flays at the path's edge like melting ice-cream.

A house, of sorts, is ten feet out from the lake's shore. The home rests on a number of poles rising out of the water. Its middle circumference is wider than the top and bottom so it slopes up and down away from an outer edge as though it where a flying saucer. Its door, a huge drawbridge, is shut tight.

The lake is long and narrow, bulging like a keyhole around the small island. A footbridge cuts across to the far bank where several rustic wooden homes are nestled among the water reeds. The path winds around the trunks' of trees along the lake's bank and out the front of red shack that might have originally been a railway freight car. A tall, skinny old man with wild silver hair each side of his bald patch, steps out of a darkened doorway, takes a brief look at me and bends down to search a pile of scrap metal.

I take a route away from the lake's shore and up onto a ridge. Dotted throughout the trees and lush undergrowth are more houses, some are mere gypsy wagons with chimneys sticking out of their roofs while others are masterpieces of craftsmanship and love, one is almost entirely constructed by a jigsaw of different sized wooden window frames. The path loops around and delivers me onto a village street with three or four terraced shops in a row. One of the shops has a sign that reads Inkoopen, and sells all kinds of things like a general store, directly opposite children run all over a playground while huge dogs laze in the sun. Beyond the children's playground several old, brown-brick, three-story buildings run parallel to the road for about eighty metres. Magnificent murals are painted across the buildings, some in the style of graffiti art, others with beautiful scenes of nature, plants and flowers in blossom. Walking among the paintings it's as though I am within the halls of a giant art gallery and I wish Carmen could see it too, she would love it.

A market area presents itself, where a small crowd drifts among the stalls buying roasted nuts, falafels, clothes, and old books. The markets narrow into a paved road, each side lined with stalls openly selling hash and ganja. Bucket size tubs of marijuana buds and blocks of hash the size of small books sit neatly on card tables. Some of the vendors are set up more permanently with wooden shelters. A few even have heating stoves for the winter. A tall black man with a wild afro cat-calls his offerings. "Acapulco Gold, Acapulco Gold. Come get it here," his table is arranged into sections of various grades and origin; hash from Afghanistan, hand rolled charis from India, Durban Poison from South Africa, and Acapulco Gold, a tightly budded strain which is priced as the most expensive. In a cookie jar are hash cookies and a bed of nails support two blends of pre-rolled joints, one for the papa bears, as his sign says, and one for the baby bears.

On the right side of Pusher Street the buildings raise up to three stories and on one of the walls are painted two big murals. The first is a big fist smashing a syringe to pieces, the second is a giant marijuana leaf. On the left I recognise the bakery from the night before. A sign above it labels it the Sunshine Bakery.

As I get closer to the main entrance of Christiania, a slow transition of the pushers becomes apparent. They are no longer smiling. The pushers at this end of the street are mostly young men with bulging muscles under their singlets and thick gold chains around their necks. Their stern faces are in constant motion moving from side to side, constantly scanning their environment. Big dogs are chained to tables protecting their masters' territory. I try not to keep eye contact with them too long and quicken my pace.

Next to the last two pusher's tables, one on either side of the street, are piles of paving stones. They are not new stones about to be laid down, but old, split and jagged as though they have been roughly pulled from the ground. Continuing along Pusher Street I recognise the rickety old barn on the right hand side and see the big Christiania sign where the taxi dropped Kidnap and me last night. On the reverse of the big sign that spans the entrance is written, *You are now entering the EU.* The contrast between the city and the village is huge. Out there is concrete, chain link fences, bitumen, traffic, pollutants, crowds, advertising and city hustle. In here are dirt tracks, green foliage, beautiful art, rustic homes and the ambling pace of village life.

Returning to the W.C. Fields Clubhouse late in the day, I find the old man, Neils, sitting out the front on a wooden bench with a bottle of Tuborg beer in his hand. His hair is almost silver and wispy thin, his cheeks shallow with a tinge of pink. He has only a slight frame and sits slouched over his legs that are crossed at the knee. Like a favourite grandfather he is gentle in soul and tender in observation. Watching my approach to the clubhouse, he says, "Hi, Hi, how was your tour? Good I hope." Picking up a beer from beside him on the bench he twists off the top, stands and hands it to me.

"I can't believe that I've never heard of this place, it's really amazing," I say.

"Sit, sit," Neils tells me as he shuffles to one side making room, "This is Poo," he says indicating a lanky guy sitting in a chair wearing big black army boots, denim jeans and a sleeveless denim jacket. He too is old with slightly orange hair and a bushy beard that is well into the process of turning grey. "And Gunner," a smaller, even older guy in a brown leather jacket raises his bottle in greeting from his chair next to Gunner. "And Larrs, over there." Larrs, a much younger guy with shoulder length straight brown hair and a craggy face says "Hi," as he raises a finger.

"So you never heard of Christiania," says Poo sharing my excitement in discovering Christiania for the first time, "It is a good place, yes?"

"Sure is, but what is it?" I ask, pleased that Poo seems happy to discuss Christiania.

"It's hard to sum up exactly what it is," Poo says as he leans back in his chair and lifts his hand to tug at stray tuffs of beard.

"Tell him how it started," suggests Gunner to Poo.

I sup at the Tuborg beer and it tastes great. The alcohol sooths my aching legs and it feels good to sit down after walking around the village for hours in constant fascination.

"Back in the early seventies, what year was it?" Poo asks for help.

"Was it '72?" suggests Gunner.

"Think so," agrees Larrs.

Poo continues. "Anyway, back in the early seventies there was a housing crisis in Denmark, most of northern Europe, I think. The government was evicting squatters and bulldozing old buildings in the city. It was hard for people to find somewhere to live, especially for those without much money or a good job. So some people broke the fence to this old Military base."

"Military base?" I say.

Gunner jumps in, obviously interested in Christiania's military history. "Yes, the area was called Badsmandsstades Kasern then. Hundreds of years ago we Danish built a massive defensive base to defend against the Swedes. There are big ramparts and defensive canals all across the north of Christiania. On the city side, to the south, are big buildings and a wall that encloses Christiania in from the city. Where we are now and further down that way are the barracks and warehouse buildings used by the army before they left."

Larrs takes up the thread, "All the gates were boarded up and the place was deserted, like a huge ghost town right in the middle of Copenhagen. People started breaking in and exploring around and then some magazine…"

"Head Magazine," says Neils.

"Head Magazine," continues Larrs. "Wrote a story about possible uses for this abandoned army base and people just started squatting here."

"We came later though," Neils says. "We weren't here until the late seventies, was it '78?"

"Round about then," Gunner says, "that was a great time for Punks at the Ark of Peace, in Christiania."

"I should tell you that we're old punks," says Neils leaning towards me with a weary smile. "We were young in the Punk days. The W.C. Fields is a punk club."

"An old punk club now," laughs Poo and they all laugh with him.

"Back then it was very different in Christiania," Gunner says returning to a more serious tone. "There was too much junk around, smack and speed. It was wild and amazing times for young punks, but people were dying, they were real dark day's man."

"All changed now though," says Larrs. "No hard drugs in Christiania, no more overdoses no more people dying."

"No more fucking biker gangs." adds Neils.

Gunner is reminded about the biker gangs, "Yeah, wow! It was real scary around here while the biker gangs were at war over the junk trade. They were killing each other. But Christiania is strong and the people held together and it is the people that survived. The junkies and bikers are all history, Christiania is free of that shit now."

"And then, of course, the government always wants to close Christiania down and evict everyone, says Poo. "I think at the moment the government's policy towards Christiania is that we are a social experiment, but really they have always wanted to get rid of us and will always want to. We will always have to keep fighting. Last year the police staked out Christiania for eight months, can you believe it? They kept us under surveillance for twenty four hours a day for eight whole months! Then they sent in the riot police, but even they couldn't get us out."

The group of old punks smile and raise their Tuborg beers, "Skol," they each say and take a deep swig.

"They try everything to get rid of us," laughs Larrs. "They say we don't pay for our electricity and water. We negotiate and start paying. They say the buildings are falling into disrepair, but when they come and look at them they find that they are well cared for."

I'm curious, "But how is it run?"

"It just runs, Christiania just happens and everything just falls into place. Life is beautiful," Larrs says smiling.

"We do have meetings. The Common Meeting is the main one. If people care what happens in Christiania they go and speak and then people argue and either agree or disagree. If most of the people agree then a decision is made. And we also have areas, like the Blue Caramel and Dussen over the lake, I think there are around ten of them in Christiania, and the people in each area decide what happens there. Like if somebody wanted to move in each person from the area would have to agree. And then, like I said, there is the Common Meeting where all the major decisions are argued about."

Larrs interrupts, "Like whether or not to pay the city for electricity and water."

"Or whether or not to go on a Love Sweden campaign," giggles Neils like a little kid.

"Love Sweden campaign?" I want to know.

"About ten years ago a right wing government was elected in Sweden and they started a smear campaign, a hate campaign, against Christiania and started to put pressure on the Danish government to get rid of us. Sweden was saying that Christiania was the root of all evil in northern Europe. I'm pretty sure that it was at a Common Meeting that Christiania decided to send a Love Army to Sweden on the Love Sweden campaign. The Love Army marched through Malmo, Goteborg and Stockholm and conquered them all with cabaret, processions, music and love."

I love it, and Gunner can see it. "You like that eh? You haven't heard about the time some people in Christiania decided that the homeless kids should get toys for Christmas. People in Christiania dressed up as Santa Claus, about twenty of them, they went into the big department stores in the city with empty sacks, lifted toys from the shelves, filled up their sacks and took the toys out to the kids living on the streets," Gunner starts to laugh and raises his voice to finish the end of the story. "Santa was on the news that night getting handcuffed and pushed to the ground by a group of really aggressive police."

"I love that kind of stuff," I say and take the final swig of my beer.

Neils hands me another.

"Oh, man, I just love Christiania," smiles Poo.

Gunner holds his Tuborg up high and says, "Skol," and we all take deep slugs of beer.

THE THIEF

Stress first thing in the morning is never good, especially when the night before has been somewhat of a bender. My head is heavy and my bones are sore and stiff. I am barely able to open my eyes and someone is yelling, "Where is she? That little bitch! I'm going to kill her!"

The cold concrete floor of the W.C. Fields Club does little to sooth my hangover as I try to understand the drama being played out by a particularly agitated young guy known as Jacob.

Last night after sitting around with the old punks from the W.C. Fields Club I found myself drinking beers at Nemoland. A girl signalled with her hand a request for a sip of the beer I was cradling. She was German and could only speak a little broken English. I speak no German beyond saying that I can't speak German, but we managed a basic communication. She carried a sleeping bag rolled into a loose wrap and I was able to understand that she had spent the previous night in a cheap hotel in Copenhagen, but now she was broke and without shelter. We smoked a joint together, shared a couple of beers and I gave her my coat when she began to shiver. The rest of her clothes were in a locker at the railway station.

We talked and drank tequila sitting around the fire in the drum in the gravel square. I was getting pretty vacant when the topic of food came up. The German girl told me she had not eaten all day. A small chunk of bread and a piece of cheese remained in my bag from the trip down from Stockholm so I fetched it for her to eat by the fire.

As she ate the alcohol washed through my body and the heat from the fire began to draw my eyes closed. Knowing the German girl had no place to sleep my conscious would not permit me to leave her alone in the night. I had a place to sleep and felt compelled to share it with her.

"Follow me?" I instructed and I turned away from the fire and wobbled towards the big ugly concrete building that is the W.C. Fields Club.

I showed her to the stairs that lead up to the loft above the kitchen, which contains a huge television and dusty old chairs and sofas. The German girl crashed out on a chair and I went to sleep downstairs on the concrete floor as the loft smells as though a thousand sweaty labourers live in it. Actually it's only two old punk guys and young Jacob who sleep up there.

"It's your fault you brought the thieving bitch back here," Jacob yells at me while I lay on the floor trying to keep the contents of my stomach from emptying on the floor.

"Oh, shit," is all I can think to say. The room spins as I attempt to edge myself up onto an elbow.

The problem, I soon discover, is that Jacob has had his favourite mamut stolen during the night, a slender, cylindrical piece of ivory used to filter joints. He's really mad and blaming me. Not only has she taken his mamut, but she also smoked Jacob's 'good morning' joint. "And she smoked my fucking joint," he keeps saying over and over again. "That mamut is worth 400 kroner, and you owe me that," he says, looking me hard in the eyes more than a little aggressively.

I know, thankfully, that the German girl is catching a train at nine thirty this morning from the central train station. I set off on a long walk into the city, hung over and not feeling particularly alive. In a daze I walk the half-hour to the train station. It takes only five minutes to find the German girl. "Hiya," I say and of course she is surprised to see me.

During the walk to the train station my mind had been preoccupied with directing my stomach not to empty itself on the city streets, so I had not formulated an angle to approach the subject of the stolen mamut. My only option is to be blunt. "You smoked a joint this morning."

She looks puzzled although I know she understands. "I catch train, must go." she replies and picks up her bags about to turn away.

"Why did you steal the mamut? You could have just smoked the joint, that would not have been so bad," I say.

"No," she says. "Why you say this, I do nothing,"

I grab at her bag thinking that I'll take it, with her following, back to Christiania and let Jacob sort through her lies. However, she is far too quick for me in my hung-over state and snatches the bag back out of my hands. "What you do this for," she protests. "I do nothing."

And for a moment I almost believe her. She senses my hesitation and suddenly seems more confident as though she's gotten away with it. I remember thinking the night before that she was running from something she appeared so desperate. "Okay," I say. "We go to the police." I grab her by the arm and begin to drag her over to a cop by the station's entrance.

"No," she protests, desperation flaring in her eyes. "I give to you, I give you the mamut, I not go police."

When I arrive back with the mamut in hand Jacob is over the moon. He looks at me as though tears are about to stream from his eyes and says, "We smoke a joint."

One of the old punks, Poo, who sleeps in the loft and who had been observing the morning, says to me, "I know where there is work in Christiania, if you're interested that is. I think they're having a meeting about it tomorrow morning."

THE MORNING PLACE

The work is at a local Christiania restaurant known as Monsters. It's actually called Morgenstedet, but the word proves too hard for me to pronounce. The Danish language sounds as if a table tennis ball is lodged firmly against the tonsils, similar to a gagging ooooo noise. When I try to pronounce the restaurant with its proper Danish sounds the old guys at the W.C. Fields Club laugh, so I've stopped trying and have settled with Monsters, which sits quite well with me and the guys only laugh half as hard.

Standing around a crate of beers out front of the W.C. Fields Club, Neils and Poo are attempting to convey directions to Monsters. With all their arm waving I am confused so I finally let out a resounding, "Ahhhhh!" as though I have all of a sudden understood their charades. I haven't but am only getting increasingly confused by all their conflicting directions. They have told me that a meeting has been scheduled at Monsters to select someone to fill a vacant position, and if I ever hope to get there in time I think it best to do so without their directions.

Leaving the guys happy with their morning beers I make off towards the gravel square, the direction indicated most frequently by Poo and Neils. Passing through, I notice a fruit and vegetable shop. A sign labels it Grøntsagen and it points me to a door in a drab brick building with a low flat roof. A concrete floor permeates a chill through a room that houses garden produce. I choose juicy pears, my favourite, and a thick crust roll from a loose pile stacked on the counter.

"Hi, hi," says a lady behind the counter. She is tall and blond and hasn't a clue that I don't speak a word of Danish. She rattles on with a friendly, positive gleam in her eyes. I don't catch her words, but I certainly catch her vibe. She's flirting with me as she sprouts the guttural sounds of Danish. She is older, perhaps forty, twice my age.

I enjoy a moment listening to the language and the enthusiastic way she speaks it then say, "Sorry, English."

She laughs, gently at first, then gradually storms into hysterics. Her hand clamps over her mouth as she realises just how loud and hearty her laugh has become. "Sorry," she says in English between gasping breaths. "I didn't think for a second that you weren't Danish."

"I'm not."

"So you're English?"

"No."

"American?"

"No."

"Ahhh," she says, seeming to have finally discovered what I am. "You're a tourist!" she laughs again. "We must be nice to the tourists," she says. "My name is Lonni. Come and have a coffee with me tonight. Come to the Kosmic Bloomst after dark."

Lonni is able to confirm my direction to the Monsters restaurant while laughing at my pronunciation. "Take the path which runs diagonally to the right of Woodstocks Bar, past the Moonfisher Café on the left and then just after the general store, Inkopen, you'll find Morgenstedet, not Monsters, on the right."

The path to the left of Woodstocks leads through a green shrouded park with tall trees, thick around their trunks. I'm heading further from the city and deeper into the village. The path turns into a gravel road as I pass the Moonfisher Café. Inside I can see people playing pool, laughing and talking with wide open faces. To the right is a long single story building that is dilapidated but obviously well used. Monsters restaurant is opposite.

Monster's has a quiet garden with a couple of heavy set wooden tables and bench seats. The building is old, but it is freshly painted and has new window frames. Yellow wagon wheels with multicoloured forks are attached to an outside wall and in between them is a large, roughly scrawled peace sign. A marijuana plant grows four feet out of a big terracotta pot placed like a sentry at the front door. A couple of rough, moulded concrete steps lead me inside where I find a small group of people sitting around three tables.

I sit and wait for something to happen. As I came here to Monsters in search of paid employment I'd invested some time earlier in cleaning and tidying myself. In the W.C. Fields Club there is a tap in the bathroom which sticks out from the wall about four feet off of the ground. I'm just over six feet so despite the fact that I can swivel the taps nozzle to spurt water out almost horizontally I still have to wash myself bent over double, attempting not to slip on the wet tiles. Unfortunately the tap issues only cold water and it really is more a trickle than a gush. It took the better part of the morning to wash and shave. The difference between me sitting here in the Monsters restaurant now and hitching highways a few days ago is large to say the least. I almost appear employable with my hair pulled back tight, the big knotty clumps held down flat against my scalp.

The oldest person in the room is a man wearing a dark brown jacket and thick glasses. Deep brow lines make him appear a thinker, while a scrawny crop of thinning hair adds a touch of worrier. Nobody says anything and there is a lot of shuffling and nail biting going on. Finally the thinker introduces himself as Jon, before suggesting that we should pull a few of the tables together and get the meeting underway. The Monster's crew introduce themselves. "Christof," says a tall, slim muscular guy of about thirty. I recognise his Israeli accent.

"Carlos," says a stereotypical looking Carlos: thick black moustache and hair, a gold medallion around his neck with the top two buttons of his shirt undone.

The final member of the Monsters crew says nothing, seemingly not impressed with the whole meeting business.

Within the group there are actually two groups. First, the staff of Monsters, four of them who spend the first few minutes of the meeting bitching about the other members who, "Could not be bothered to get out of bed to come to the meeting."

The second group, which I am a part of, are those who are here about the job. There are six hopefuls, ten in the meeting all together. The two groups sit at opposite ends of the tables facing each other. No-one seems to know how to start the meeting so we are all engulfed by an awkward silence. A couple of the Monsters crew retreat to safety and once again start their bitching about lazy colleges who didn't bother turning up to the meeting. Carlos pulls a rough patch of leather, about fifteen centimetres in diameter, from his pocket and begins to crumble a block of hash onto its worn surface.

"I think," says Jon, the thinker, with a rather eccentric postulation. "That the best way to go about this is for me to describe the situation at Morgenstedet. After that we can hear from each of you in regards to why you want to work here. I hope there is no objection to speaking in English as there a few present who don't speak Danish."

No-one minds enough to say anything out loud, but I sense a slight air of hostility from some of the Danes.

"Okay, so we are in spring," says Jon, "And I for one are very happy about this and am looking forward to acquainting myself with warmth once again. Spring means busy people. Yes, and many more people in Christiania, all those tourists coming to see the freaks." He laughs, or rather giggles, seeming to enjoy the freak label.

"Okay so we need at Morgenstedet, one, maybe two extra people throughout the summer to help. That's why we are here today," he indicates to my group at the end of the table.

"At Monsters there are no bosses. There are no rules. We just want to find someone who'll be able to work with us with as few problems as possible."

Carlos is roasting a cigarette over a lighter's flame.

"I would like a job," says an Italian woman sitting next to me, quite abruptly, but then again she is Italian and I don't quite understand the passion and mystery of Italians. Jon, however doesn't seem too impressed with her interjection.

"Oh you do, do you?" he asks her quite seriously looking up at the Italian over his glasses while tilting his head down.

The Italian woman doesn't seem to realise her mistake and continues, "I can cook, I'm great at tables. I need the money. I'll do anything!"

"Hmmmm," is the only response Jon offers to her outburst.

The next two girls who speak are both Danish and one says she worked at Monsters a year or so earlier. Her name is Kat. Both Kat and the other Danish girl say pretty much the same thing. They have been travelling for the past couple of years and want a little extra cash. Both seem at ease with the Monsters crew.

Carlos ejects a sweet smelling cloud of smoke across the table. A huge joint pokes out from between his right pinkie and ring fingers. He cups his left hand underneath to form an airtight seal against his lips, breathes deeply and blows another cloud of smoke across the table. The joint then travels around the group, landing with me just as it appears to be my turn to pitch for the job. I take a toke then hand the joint back to Carlos.

Standing up I'm not exactly sure what to say so I simply relate the events of the past couple of weeks that have brought me to Christiania and into the W.C Fields club. Carlos chokes while toting on his joint and begins to cough uncontrollably which brings my pitch to an abrupt end.

Next up is a wiry little guy who looks as though he is about twenty years older than he probably is. His face is cragged with deep lines and slack skin loosely hangs from his cheek bones. His head is large, disproportionate to his narrow shoulders and slight frame. I can't help but think he looks like a hardboiled egg in a small cup. As he begins to speak the rest of us lean in attempting to understand what he is saying. I initially think he must be speaking Danish, but the quizzical faces of the group's Danish speakers show that he obviously isn't. After an unintelligible sentence or two I gradually begin to decipher the odd word until I slowly realise that he is in fact speaking English with an incredibly thick Scottish accent. "...L'ke I boon 'er fa a while nu an' I 'ave nu cash l'ft. I nad a job. Ma name tis Gregg." And, having had his say, he sits back down as members of the Monsters collective look at each other trying to register if any of them understood a word of what he said.

Gregg seems to sense that he wasn't understood and a slight flicker of despair appears in his eyes before it is quickly replaced by the sharp glare of anger. I empathise with him, another stranger in a strange land, so I say, "Hi Gregg, I'm running out of cash too," and this seems to cool the anger that flared so quickly.

The last hopeful to present himself doesn't seem to care too much about the job. Not having washed or shaved as I have, he wears old, raggedy clothes covered with a thick, black leather jacket. His hair, sculpted from sleep, stands up in tuffs all over his head. His eyes seem not to have adjusted to the daylight yet and squint as he speaks softly, "I'm not doing too much else these days and I guess I'm looking for a reason to get out of bed." He receives the joint and stops speaking while he slowly takes a long toke and passes it on. "I dunno, I'm here, you know me, I know you, give it to one of these others if they need the work, but otherwise I'm happy to help. A little more money would be nice."

The Monsters crew sit silent for a moment, contemplating their next move. A move that will affect their enjoyment of the coming season's warmth, as it is clear that they are interviewing us based on personality rather than skills and experience.

"Okay," says Jon, who appears to be the non-boss. "I have come to a decision."

Carlos and Christof glare at him. "No, wait, don't look at me like that," he replies in response to their glares.

"You have made a decision?" booms Christof, not actually shouting, but his voice is very low and deep and resonates within the room.

Carlos blows a smoke ring in Jon's direction, also not impressed with the fact he has made a decision without consulting the others in the collective.

Christof continues, "I would like to hear this decision of yours seeing that it is to be mine as well."

"Yes, you're about to and you'll think it's fair if you'd give me the chance," declares Jon.

Christof sits back in his chair spreading his massive arms apart offering the podium back to Jon.

"The decision I would like to propose," he looks to Christof for approval of his wording.

Christof nods, not entirely happy and still sitting with his arms crossed, but he's giving Jon the go ahead.

"I suggest that we put all of your names into a hat then draw them out. The order they are drawn will be the order that you will each come in for three or four days to work at Morgenstedet. I think that this is the only way to see who is truly best suited for our group."

Christof begins to shake his head.

"You don't agree?" asks Jon in a conciliatory tone, obviously aware that he is on thin ice with Christof's temper.

"I think it is unfair," I can feel Christof's voice in my chest cavity it is so deep and resonates so strongly. "These people are here for work, they need to know. What you say will take two weeks, probably longer. You say they can come in and work for three or four days, whatever, then the next person and so on for six people, meanwhile none can know where they stand."

"Well then," Jon becomes defensive of his idea. "What do you propose?"

"I think we should decide now."

We hopefuls at the table are forgotten for the moment as the Monsters crew argue at the other end of the table. Not about which one of us they want to join their collective, but on the method to be used in order to determine that decision. Ten minutes later no decision has been made and the meeting is declared closed. We are all told to drop by over the next couple of weeks to do a bit of trial work. No exact days or times are offered.

"Oh, if any of you have no money and are hungry you can drop by to work for food anytime," says Carlos as we all stand to leave.

As I walk out of Monsters past the potted marijuana plant I have no idea what the deal on the job is.

"Hey, wait op thar yunun!" shouts out Gregg, the Scotsman, from a few paces behind. "I huv no gut mach, ba lets smoke a spliff, eh? Those tossas wa fook'n rude lyke, but noo you. Ya a god mun. Sit har and smoke thus." And as he catches up he produces a tiny block of hash.

We sit on the edge of the dirt road and lean back against the wall of Monsters while Gregg starts to roll a pitifully small joint. I have a little hash too so I add it into his mix to make the joint a little more worthwhile. "I wanta go back ta Glasgow and start ma own place like Christiania. Its fookin grand init?"

"I've only been here a week and I love it already," I add to Gregg's excitement.

"A wek, I bun hare a fookin month, lyke. I noo 'bout thus place antis well good. I doon rally wont to fookin wak, but ah 'ave nu cash, wakin's fa fools and fookin hourses," says Gregg spitefully while staring intensely into my eyes.

I recognise him, not him in person, but in type. I've met a lot of Scots from Glasgow and many seem constantly trying to prove themselves as hard men through endless fighting and one-up man ship, career criminals borne from generations of poverty living under the boots of their British overlords. To be fair on the Glaswegians though, it's not just them. I've seen the same attitudes among the Skousers from Liverpool and the Geordies from Newcastle. It's the north of England where people have been ill-treated by the system for centuries, a whole underclass of underprivileged who are hell-bent on shafting those the system favours, but really anyone who appears to them to be well off. The type I've met before, the type I see in Gregg, are dangerous if you cross them and the first step to crossing them is to get to know them.

"Daya 'ave a flame?" asks Gregg having rolled the joint.

I pass him my cigarette lighter and it doesn't surprise me in the least that he pockets it after sparking the joint. I let it go though as I have another and all I can think about is how to extract myself from his presence once the joint is smoked. Gregg rattles on in his barely decipherable accent, a never ending rant of whatever seems to come into his mind. I can understand only about a third of what comes out of his mouth, which is barely enough to get a general idea of what he is saying. As I piece together his ranting I am further convinced of the need to make my exit as quickly as possible. "...fookin screws an jail wa well evil lyke an I dun wan ta go buk thar..."

His thoughts take twists and turns through various tangents and back again until he has talked himself in circles, "...sa I jus had to shive her lyke, fookin slat..."

I tune out, nodding and grunting where he expects me to so as not to make him angry, "...nu wat I men, tay all should be fookin kalled?"

Nod.

"...fookn twats, well d'served, eh?"

Grunt.

I watch the street life of Christiania walk by. As soon as he stubs the last of the joint out in the dirt I make an excuse of having to meet someone. Gregg seems a little offended by my quick departure, but nonetheless seems to accept that I have to go. Relieved that I've escaped without inciting Greg into an act of violence, I head back to the W.C Fields Club to drink beer with Poo and Gunner in the warm afternoon sun.

LONNI

"The Kosmic Bloomst?" I ask a dog on the path outside the Moonfisher café. "The Kosmic Flower." I reiterate, but still the dog does not understand me. It looks at me and tilts its head slightly as if to say, "Dog, stupid, I only speak dog!"

The Kosmic Bloomst is where Lonni lives, the Cosmic Flower. The dog's trying to understand, I can see the effort he's putting in. His head tilts from side to side and he gawks at me. I walk past the dog leaving him to his little patch of territory and towards the bridge that crosses the small lake. As I move away from the centre of the village the night is absolutely black and the only way I can keep on the path is to feel for the cracking bitumen beneath my feet. At times it disappears and I walk into unseen bushes. The lights of the city shine not far away but don't intrude on this little village haven. A bike approaches from behind with its rider periodically ringing its bell and as it races by I yell out for directions, "The Kosmic Bloomst?"

"Turn right after the bridge, the last building," yells the rider already five metres ahead.

How can he see? He must be hurtling through total blackness guided by memory alone.

About two hundred metres to the right after the bridge I find the last building. On a wood board is written, The Kosmic Bloomst, in big, colourful letters. The road continues around the left side of the building, but I take a narrow path to the right that runs between the side of the building and the lake. The Kosmic Bloomst is one of four identical buildings on this side of the lake. Shaped as an L, it is about thirty metres on each side with thick stone walls that must have been laid at least three or four hundred years ago, but still very sturdy. The A-frame roof is steep with attic windows on both sides. Rounding the side of the building the path opens up to a grassed courtyard with a brick fire hole in its centre. To the right is the lake only ten metres away. I knock on a thick, rustic door and hear footsteps coming down stairs. The door swings open to reveal Lonni, smiling.

"It's the tourist," she teases me. Her smile is huge with her mouth opening wide to reveal pearly white teeth.

"Hi, hi," I say to her.

"Coffee or whisky?" she asks.

"Whisky I say," preferring coffee, but Lonni caught me off guard with the question as I was surveying her beauty, a hard, rough type of beauty. She pours the whisky straight up into a tumbler glass, almost overflowing it.

As she hands it to me, Lonni makes towards a wide set of steep stairs that twist their way up into the attic. I follow her up into the darkness. The roof is steeply angled so I am forced to duck my head, which tips my balance, and I fall up the stairs spilling more than a few drops of whisky. "Shit!" I yell, accompanied by a loud thud.

"Shhhhhhh," Lonni raises a finger to her lips and is looking down at me less than pleased. "My daughters are asleep down there."

I peek my head below the floorboards and deep in the darkness I can see a huge four-poster bed. Two lumps are covered by a quilt and I can make out blonde hair like Lonni's. Hair so blond and shiny it almost glows in the dark.

In the loft, Lonni has a few candles burning and continues to light more. Thick beams of ancient wood run across the room at shoulder height. Lonni is almost as tall as I am and she's bobbing up and down under the beams as she crosses the room. A mess of children's toys is strewn at the far end of the attic. In the middle of the space is a large, beaten table that divides the considerable space. Lonni and I sit on a couple of boxes surrounded by a sphere of candlelight that projects our shadows onto the sloping roof. "So you have two daughters," I begin, awkwardly initiating conversation.

"Nin and Franny, Nin's twelve and Franny's six. I also have a son. He's a young man, but he's straight." As she says the word 'straight' her right hind slices vertically away from her forehead mimicking a shark's fin above the water. "He lives with his father in the city." She pauses for a moment, thinking and adds, "I need to leave here…go… back to the city to be straight." The shark's fin goes for another swim out from her forehead. "Become normal. My girls are growing up, Nin is about to start menstruating and we don't even have a toilet or bathroom. She'll need these things soon. Life is hard in Christiania. In the city life is easy, people will say it isn't, but it is. In the city you have a toilet and hot water. In the summer it's not so bad here, just strip your clothes off and hang a hose over the tree, but in the winter…maybe I'd rather be in the country, just live in a tent, just me and my girls and a forest. I just want to go, you know?" she seeks confirmation.

"Yeah, I know." I say to her.

She questions, "Do you?"

"Well, of course I don't know how you feel, but I just wanted to go too, leave the city and get away."

"Christiania has a habit of kidnapping people."

"Yeah, I've discovered that already," then tell her how I arrived.

"A regular Jack Kerouac," she laughs when I'm finished and I blush for the compliment.

"That's exactly what I want, just to get up and leave, go somewhere," she sighs. "But I have my girls and I can't. I have responsibilities"

It's an endless argument for her and there's no answer. As though she wants to avoid the complexity of her problems she changes the subject. "Where are you staying?"

"In Christiania."

"Where?"

"Oh," and I laugh at having to tell her as I am not used to the name yet. "At the W.C. Fields Club house."

"Argggh. That horrible place, the men's club!" As she says this she pulls a disgusted face.

"I've never heard it being called that," I say.

"Well, have you ever seen any women there? I shouldn't be so hard on those guys. They have done some good things in Christiania and I guess I owe them some sort of thanks for the place."

"They are good guys. They've helped me a lot. I think you're so lucky to be living here," I tell her, wide eyed in my excitement. "It is such a beautiful place. Like a little country village, a crazy little village, smack bang in the middle of a city."

"Lucky?" she says sarcastically. "Lauuucky," she says again with that awkward balled Danish sound from deep in her throat. A sound, I'm sure, that only a Dane can make. "I've hardly been lucky in Christiania."

"No?"

"To begin with," she says, not complaining, but stating. "Only a week ago my lover took all my money and never came back. Not to be seen again"

"Your lover?" Lonni had strongly emphasised the love within the word.

"For almost four years we stayed in bed making love. He wasn't always around, but most of the time he was. We had it so right. We were like this," and she crosses two of her fingers and holds them up in the candlelight. She squeezes them together with what seems all her force and they tremble. A tear appears in her eye, but she blinks it away. Her tongue pokes out from the side of her mouth to initiate a crazy face and then she crosses her eyes and laughs.

"I don't understand," says Lonni, holding her head low and slowly shaking it. "He took my money. I can understand that, but he also took a pair of my underwear and my girls Lego! My underwear, I can almost understand that…" she pauses for a moment and feigns a shiver. "I don't know if I like it, in a way I do," a sly smile slides across her lips. "But it's also a little off. Don't you think?"

"Were they clean?" I ask.

Lonni smiles and stares at me blankly, then laughs. It all seems a little too rude. She punches me lightly on the shoulder and almost falls off of the box when the laughter reaches her belly and shakes her body. Whether it is the whisky or that Lonni just hasn't laughed for a while I don't know, but she's thoroughly enjoying the experience, despite the painful memories of her lover. Quite suddenly she stops laughing and says, "The Leeego, that is what I don't understand. Why did he take my girls Leeego?" Her accent stretches the 'e'. "It wasn't like he ever played with it while he lived here. He was a strange one though," she says, serious again. "I'll tell you that, but he's a genius, a spiritual genius. I know he is, but it seemed as though only I could ever know his true brilliance. He was so beautiful; he wouldn't speak, only sing, wonderfully."

"He could sing, but not talk?" I question, fascinated with Lonni and the way she talks and expresses herself.

"The only way he'd really communicate was by singing. He'd say that words stole his true meaning. That words were totally inadequate as they had predefined meanings and the only way to truly communicate was through the artistic emotion of song and singing and dancing and painting. If he did say something to me, which was rare, he'd always remind me that they weren't his words and not to trust them, but that's the least of it. Once he was dragged off to hospital after sitting naked on an armchair downstairs for three days proclaiming himself to be God. I sort of understood what he meant. It was kind of a joke. I thought it was funny, but they came and got him and took him away. There were things about him that were…indescribable, wonderful. And I miss him, we were soul mates." A tear escapes Lonni's eyelashes and streams down her cheek without her even noticing.

She stands and walks into the darkness to stare out the window above the stairs. I sense her pain as it seeps out, I can feel that she wants, or rather needs, to share it with me. "I miss him," she says softly. "It's as though a piece of me is missing, gone. And I don't know where and I don't think that I will ever get it back again."

We sit in silence for some time before a twitch turns Lonni's sullen lips into a sudden smile. "Why the Lego?" she says.

Before we can wonder why we are both laughing, big hearty laughs that cramp my stomach. Lonni's pain has been so thick in the room that suddenly there is no more room left for it. It is contradictory and inexplicable, but that's what we do, laugh and laugh. No more crying, just laughing.

"Shhhhh, my girls!" Lonni is trying to be angry with me, but she can't contain a runaway smile.

It's well past midnight when I walk around the lake back to the village centre and the W.C. Fields Clubhouse. Several tall whiskies, a joint or two, the wash of Lonni's emotional pain and a belly ache from all the laughter have made my steps heavy and ill-directed. A smile across my lips arches up to a recent moon and a grey night sky that blows about reassuringly in a strong breeze. I'm happy to have somewhere to go, a direction after drifting across the freeways of Sweden, even if it is just a cold, hard floor at the smelly clubhouse.

JAIL

I startle awake. People are organising, dragging things about and shouting to each other in Danish. The floor is cool, which is nice as the sun shines bright and hot through the windows, heating my face and bathing my body in a slight film of perspiration. I continue to lie in my bag allowing the stiffness in my muscles time to stretch out as I squirm around. Rolling onto my stomach I catch Jacob walking by on the other side of the clubhouse. "What's the time?" I shout out to him.

He's busy, on some kind of a mission, but stops for a moment to look at me bewildered. "The time, hell I don't know. What do you want to know a silly thing like that for," he says agitated by the question.

And why do I want to know? Jacob's already moved on leaving me feeling a little silly for the question. Time, I wonder, stuffing my bag away and rolling up my sleeping mat, just an artificial construct of the human mind. I notice a large gathering of people just outside the clubhouse.

Having splashed water over my face and scraped the snot from my eyes I join the people outside who are lavishing healthy swigs of beer. The sun's strength has only just started asserting itself, a little less than a quarter up the sky.

"What's going on?" I ask Poo, one of the clubhouse regulars who sleeps in the loft.

"Today we are saying farewell to Neils," Poo tells me with a beer in his hand and I can tell it's not his first or probably even his second.

"Farewell to Neils? Where's he off to?"

Poo has just enough time to say, "Jail," before a five foot long, wood-carved chillum is pushed his way.

To take his toke, Poo is forced to kneel on the ground while two others support the chillum. One holds the base while another stretches high to stabilise its height. From this kneeling position Poo nods he is ready. A third guy holds a cigarette lighter over the chillum's gaping mouth where a huge quantity of hash and roasted tobacco has been tightly packed. Poo puffs madly on the mouth piece just as he would fire up an old pipe, except he has to stretch his mouth very wide to cover the hole at the bottom. Poo breathes in a lungful and struggles to hold it in and then blows great bilious clouds of smoke out the side of his pursed lips. In quick succession he repeats this three, then four times. Five feet above Poo's strained, upturned face a bursting flame shoots a foot into the air each time he stops drawing breath. Sweet-smelling smoke billows from the end of the long pipe as though it's coming from a factory's furnace stack. Standing slowly, Poo wobbles and restrains a cough with grunting and twitching.

When he is composed he continues, "Yeah, It's funny you know, Neils going to jail."

"Funny?" I say, not sure how it could be.

"Yeah," Poo's smiling. "The jail that he's off to is in the country, among the woods and trees. You know that Neils is a woodcarver, yes? In among the trees is his prison!" Poo laughs at this. "There is more hash out there in the woods than in Christiania."

I laugh too, doubting what Poo tells me. More hash than in Christiania? Everywhere I look I see joints and chillums flicking into life and there are chunks of hash the size of house bricks displayed on the tables in the market stalls.

"It's true," he reassures me seeing the doubt in my expression. "Plenty of hash, but no beer. That is why we're having a day of it today, for a change." He laughs at his own joke for they are always drinking beer at the W.C. Fields Club. "Three meals a day, good people to talk to, an imaginary line drawn in the forest and plenty of wood to carve." Poo turns to Neils, "Hey Neils, don't you go crossing that line!"

"As if I could see the damned thing!" Neils replies, not far from being blind drunk. "In the country for me son," he slurs, "And all for a lousy 250 grams of hash, which wasn't even mine. I'm innocent. Don't go carrying hash in the train station, that's the moral of my story. How are you?"

"Fine," I tell him, sorry that he won't be around for a while.

Neils slings an arm around me and hangs his drunken weight off of my shoulder. "I'm glad to see that you're staying in Christiania," he says. "It's too good a place for you to just pass through."

Poo and Gunner are laughing and making cooing faces at Neils' sentimental drunkenness. "I think he loves you," chuckles Gunner.

"Shut up you old dirt bag!" yells Neils, sloshing his beer at Gunner in an attempt to splash him.

"I don't understand," I say to the tiny old man cradled under my arm. "Why are you even going to jail? I thought the police couldn't get at you in Christiania?"

"They can't," Neils pauses for a long burp that leaves his bottom lip glistening with spit. "They can't, but the life of a fugitive is not for an old man like me, eh?"

I still don't understand. "But if you just stay in Christiania you're not really a fugitive are you? Can't you just stay here and avoid the police?"

Neils unlatches his arm from around my shoulder and immediately loses his balance, crashing into the front wall of the W.C. Fields Clubhouse. By the time he has regained his balance another of club regulars embraces him and they both cheer and take long swigs from their beers. Neils is gone from the conversation, but Poo is happy to take over. "Neils is on a pension; me too. If we want to keep getting our money we need to go out into the city to get it. Sure he could avoid jail by just never leaving Christiania, but then he would stop getting his money from the government. Guys like us, old guys, need our pensions. It's the only money we have."

"Is everyone in Christinia taking money from the government?" I ask.

"Not everyone. Some do, some don't. It is a big argument really. Many people say that by taking the government's money we allow for the government to think it has the right to have a say in what goes on in here. I think they are right; we shouldn't take the government's money. It would be better if we didn't, but I'm an old man and just want to drink beer and be left in peace."

Gunner's been listening in and can see the disappointment on my face. "There are many people who aren't taking the government's money. There are lots of artists and musicians who make their own money and many businesses in Christiania do pretty well for themselves."

Poo interjects, "Christiania Bikes, Loppen Nightclub, the Moonfisher, the Green Hall. There are plenty of successful businesses in Christiania; you could hardly count them all."

Gunner continues, "Plus all the pushers make good money. Anyway, in Christiania you don't need lots of money to live. Who cares about money?"

"I can see that you are a little disappointed that we take the government's money," says Poo. "Perhaps we aren't the best example of Christiania for a young guy like you."

I'm silent for a moment, wondering if I have the right to judge these old men who want nothing more than to be a part of a club and drink beers in the morning sunshine. "Who am I to judge? The world isn't perfect, right?"

"To lazy old men," laughs Gunner raising his beer. "Skoll."

Poo lifts his beer. "Lazy old men."

And they both take long draws of their beers.

Not wanting to get involved in Neil's beer swilling and giant chillum smoking farewell so early in the morning I make my way through the gravel square, past Nemoland and into Grøntsagen for breakfast. Lonni smiles at me. The pain I witnessed last night has vanished from her eyes, replaced by the sparkle of positivity. "My tourist!" she remarks as I enter.

I smile at the label and pull an imaginary camera from a pocket in my leathers and begin to take happy snaps of dented brown pears stacked on a shelf. "You'll come and see the slides of my holiday, won't you?"

Lonni's smile turns into a laugh and she asks me to join her on the other side of the counter where a steaming mug of coffee waits on a table. She makes a second mug for me. We talk the morning through while people come and go. Bums buying bread rolls, swigging from beers while waiting on Lonni to make out change, mothers with prams, a couple of Rastafarians, a curious dog. I munch on breakfast apples and pears and Lonni, wonderful woman, slips me a samosa free of charge.

"I must apologise for last night. I went on and on," she says, extending her words which are thick with the gruff Danish guttural throat sound that I find impossible to emulate. "Oooonnn and oooonnn!"

I know that she is talking about her pain and her vanished singing, underwear and Lego-thieving lover.

"I'm just so consumed by it all at the moment. Not a moment passes when I'm not thinking about him. No more though. With you I will be straight," and the shark fin comes swimming out from her forehead propelled by her arm. "Last night was good for me. I haven't laughed like that for so long. It was fun having a tourist around. And I've been thinking, the clubhouse where you're staying is awful, dirty, drab, nothing but grey concrete. And those men! It mustn't be very nice sleeping there."

"They're okay, good guys and they've taken care of me," I shrug my shoulders. I hadn't really thought about the awfulness of the place, just thankful for having somewhere to stash my bags and a secure place to sleep where I don't have to fear the rain and a foot in the side wake up call. "Actually, I think I'm quite lucky."

"Luaaaaaacky!" she exclaims tipping her head back as her smile gapes wide. "Ha, perhaps you'd prefer my attic at the Kosmic Bloomst?"

"Luaaaaaaacky," I mimic her. "I think I'm very lauuuucky. I've been here only a week and already I've places to stay and friends to look out for me."

"I finish here soon, how about lunch?"

"Maybe," I reply still thinking about her offer of the attic in the Kosmic Bloomst.

Lonni acts offended, "Oh, so the honour of lunch with you is never certain is it?"

"What, sorry, I was thinking of your attic."

"Oh."

"But I'll see you for lunch. Where?"

"You know Morgenstedet?"

"Yeah, I know Monsters," I say.

"Monsters!' Lonni laughs out loud again.

"Yeah, I can't pronounce it properly." I try to pronounce it but feel like a fool as I murder the Danish language.

Lonni can't stop chuckling at my attempts to get my mouth and throat around the 'ooo' sounds of the Danish language.

"You know," she says. "That Morgenstedet, means *the morning place* and by you calling it Monsters it kills that meaning entirely. I'll see you at Monsters in an hour then." She places a special emphasis on the word Monsters.

And I leave her to the morning fruit and vegetable trade.

MONSTERS

The small birds of Christiania chirp their songs and busily flutter about building their nests in the trees outside of Monsters. The dogs appear to be smiling. Huge Great Danes laze about in the sun, their immense size obstructing entire roads. With tongues hanging out and their eyes closed they appear not to notice the people stepping over. The small dogs bark, a continuous yapping, quite a contrast to the massive Great Danes who lay silent but for their deep rumbling breaths. The dogs in Christiania seem to live by a different rule book to those out in the city. With their bold strutting, rude obstructing and insistent yapping they appear more wild than tame. Over the past-twenty five years these dogs appear to have emancipated themselves from human serfdom. I'm sure that that Great Dane over there by the marijuana plant considers no human his master. I can't imagine him lapping at anyone's feet mindlessly barking 'You're the boss, anything you say master.' No, that dog, that great big fucking Dane I am sure is his own dog.

I recognise Carlos from the Monsters meeting a couple of days ago. He's a tidy man. Among the rustic people and places of Christiania, Carlos manages to look as though he just stepped out of the city, having popped in from the straight world to say 'hi' to the multitude of different creeds that make up the populace of Christiania. And there's Christof, big as ever, with defined, sinewy arms that thrust a wooden spoon around a large mixing bowel. Despite his size Christof looks meek like a child waiting for confirmation of a good deed done or a scalding for being naughty. "Hi, hi," he shouts out to me through the open door. "Always add the salt to the potatoes as the last thing. That's how you make the perfect mashed potatoes."

I watch these two go about their work from outside where I sit at a garden bench in the small courtyard.

Lonni arrives and greats me with, "Hi, hi!"

She's smiling, absolutely beaming. "Looking radiant," I remark and she blushes.

"You know," she says. "I've been thinking. How about you and I rob a bank? Then I'll have money for a bathroom and a new window."

"Yeah sure, tomorrow, I feel like a rest today."

Together we step into Monsters and I ask Christof to ladle me a bowel of cauliflower soup. Lonni chooses a seaweed salad. "Are you coming to work with us?" Christof asks in his deep voice. Even though he speaks gently it's as though we're in a tunnel and his voice is bouncing around an enclosed area.

"I don't know, you tell me, am I?"

"No, no," Christof shakes his head slowly. "It's really up to you, just come in sometime and wash some dishes then have something to eat. Start like this. So, I'll ask you again, give you a second chance. Are you coming to work with us?"

"I guess I am." I make my mind up to like Christof. The juxtaposition of his great size, muscularity and booming voice to the friendly, gentle soul within attracts me greatly.

I only spill a portion of the soup walking back out to the garden bench. When we're seated, Lonni says to me, "You know, this is the first time I've been back to Morgenstedet since he left."

Of course she's talking about her lover. "Why, did something happen here?" I sensed that something had.

"Yes," pain creeps back into her eyes. "When he left, the Leeego and my underwear were not the only things to go missing. He was working here at Monsters as a cook and he stole some money from them. I'm not sure how much, but I think it was a lot. This is the first time I've had the courage to come back."

The pain evident in her eyes recedes slightly, beaten back by a whisper of hope. Her gaze is to the future. "Thanks," she says to me.

"I've done nothing," I protest. "Lonni, we've only just met. You're the one helping me!"

"Yes I know thaaaaaat! You're good for me though, that I already know. When you came into Grøntsagen the other day I saw new energy. Wonderful new energy in you and I decided to take advantage of it, of you."

"Well, I'll just have to use you back and live in your attic, won't I?"

"Tomorrow you move in," she smiles, her pain forgotten.

Carlos comes to sit down at the table. Not actually to join us, just to eat his lunch. Lonni's head dips and her shoulders sag. She's no longer smiling and doesn't seem to want to talk. From his breast pocket Carlos draws a plastic baggie containing pot and lays out his small circle of leather, breaking up the flower bud. "My good friend from back home in South Africa sent me this. Durban poison," he says to both me and Lonni with a smile. "Grows in the fields next to a Nuclear power plant. Good stuff!"

Lonni still doesn't look up. I'm guessing that she feels responsible for the money that her lover stole. "How long have you been in Christiania?" I ask Carlos not knowing what else to say.

"How long?" Carlos repeats. "Couldn't tell you, longer than you and I only say that because you ask such a question. Time doesn't exist anymore for me while I'm here. You'd be better off asking me how long haven't I been in Christiania. That I know the answer to: too long. Life doesn't begin at thirty. No, life begins at Christiania," He laughs.

Carlos sparks up the joint. Hardly drawing on it he calls out Lonni's name as though she's an old friend and passes the joint to her, a peace offering. What could have been your everyday joint to rid a soul of time has become a deliberate act of reconciliation. Carlos smiles at Lonni, who takes the joint from his reaching hand. Lonni smiles too.

"Work," says Carlos to me, suddenly changing the subject and breaking the awkward, but friendly moment. "Have you found any?"

"No, but Christof was saying I should come in some time."

"You should, any time you want, absolutely, dishes for food. There's a deal, any time you're hungry. What we really need though is a Danish speaking food server. Sorry, but that's what we need." He smiles in matter-of-fact fashion. "Next week we may have one day for you. A spring clean seeing that it's spring." He laughs again thinking that he is funny and appears to wonder why I'm only smiling and not laughing at his joke. "It might take a day to give the place a good clean. Clean everything, you know, everything off of the shelves, in the cupboards, for a day, perhaps 300 kroner."

So there's work to be had at Monsters. Right now, however, my belly is filling with warm cauliflower soup.

PUSHER STREET

Night rests on Christiania and with it comes the city folk. After five o'clock, when the whistle blows and the city slaves are released from their shackled grind, Pusher Street comes alive. It's as though all of Copenhagen comes to buy and smoke hash. People of every age, any description, they all descend on the Free Town to sample its taste of freedom. Not simply the hash and grass, that's just the surface of it, the obvious. They come to take refreshment from a deeper substance that is to be found here within the anarchic rawness of village life. They come to experience a life, a world, without rules, without boundaries, without structure; a life that oozes massive creativity and a crude, primordial energy. I watch people walk under the Christiania sign, stepping out of the city and leaving the European Union behind: a man in a business suit, a briefcase for his stash; a couple of teenagers with pimples and a construction worker in a jumpsuit. An old lady shuffles in followed by a kid who is barely in his teens, then a couple on a date. An apparently endless procession of taxis deposits them at the gate of the Free Town. They all come and I'm watching them as I sit on Pusher Street's dirt shoulder just down from Christiania's main gate. I watch and I write with my notepad thrust up against my knee. A stream of consciousness flows through the pencil onto the page and as one stream comes to an end I look up to see an old man strolling past. He catches my gaze and from the wisdom of age to the exhilaration of youth he slights his head to one side, offering me an encouraging wink. I'm inspired and a new stream begins scrawled messily across the page within my notebook:

> Dirty, filthy stinking
> Old man passes winking
> Time for a smile
> As he walks on by
> And leaves me to my thinking
> Dirty, filthy Stinking

Excuse me sir
Do you have the time?
I ask as I've lost mine
And as you say
Please, also the day
The date?
Yes I'm always late

I lose the time with ease
As my mind becomes daydream winking
As I sit
Dirty, filthy stinking

With the clean crisp city folk walking past I realise, alive to the contrast, that I do in fact need a bath. The taxis keep coming and more people are delivered. They hurry to get out and they rush to get in, half jogging or walking at a quick pace into Pusher Street. The straighter they appear the faster they walk. It's been more than a week since I came through that gate, in amazement, also delivered by a taxi. Flicking a cigarette butt towards the city I stand defiant like David before the giant. The city is still ugly, to me, and it heaves with all its corralled masses, but no longer seems as powerful as it once did. It is now of another world, a world that hardly matters, a world that Christiania keeps at bay like a bouncer to an exclusive nightclub. The big sign, the front gate of Christiania, keeps the straight world's attitudes, values and ambitions out. In here careers and mortgages and new cars do not exist and there are no haves and have-nots, no winners, no losers, no Jones's to keep up with and no measure of success to peg myself against. I feel free of all that city shit as though it has been quarantined on the other side of Christiania's main gate.

Both sides of Pusher Street host a throng of activity. A market scene lies before me like a perspective drawing, all big and consuming in the foreground then disappearing towards Grøntsagen over the top of the crowd's headline. These pushers at the start of Pusher Street are hard-looking men with big muscles and tattoos. If it weren't for all the city folk streaming in it would be easy to forget the desire to be clean among these men. Their hair straggles and their fingernails are chipped and stained.

Sitting high on stools cemented into the dirt they are the first to survey the people entering the Free Town. Some of the city folk who visit Christiania venture no further than this first line of pushers, wanting their hash and nothing more than to just get in and out as fast as possible. And if they have only ever ventured as far as this first line of shabby, menacing pushers then it's easy to understand why they have no desire to go any further. The vibe is decidedly aggressive and uninviting, a deceptive veil to the magic that lies deeper within the Free Town. These front line pushers snarl and menacingly postulate as their dogs strain against the thick chains that hold them, bareing teeth at the city folk.

They have noticed me, the pushers, they have seen that I'm hanging around and watching. Their eyes dart around, up towards the city anticipating the incoming mass of dollars to their pockets, then back to me, an unknown in an environment that is theirs by right of intimidation. I'm watching lots of money change hands followed by the dispensing of hash, an illegal substance out in the city. And they're watching me watching them. I catch contact with a particularly callous set of eyes set deep under the brow of a well-beaten and scarred face. The eyes say, "Fuck off."

A dog barks and snaps his chain tight as he lunges towards me. I slink back away from the city and deeper into Christiania away from the front gate, the menacing pushers and the straight world.

"Buy your hash, good hash! Grass, pot, Mali Wanni from Hawaii, Thailand, Mexico. Buy a joint, buy a gram, buy an ounce, only the best!"

There is big John with his afro standing high, catcalling his wares. I walk over to see what he has, as he boasts he has pot from everywhere. "Malli Wanni!" he yells as though it is today's hot news, stretching his words as much as his smile. With skin blacker than the night he seems to glisten under the moon. His hair is just so large, like a parody sixties magazine photo it balloons about his head and drifts and sways in the breeze. He has noticed me gawking and capitalises on the opportunity. "Bro-ther, you look like you're looking, a pre-rolled joint perhaps? A hash cookie? Maybe some Acapulco Gold?"

His eyes are kind and his style infectious. I can't help but like him, although he doesn't remember me from my first day. I guess he is simply doing too much business to remember faces.

"Yeah, I guess I could be interested in some of your Mali Wani," I mimic committing myself to a sale.

"The best deals in town, bro-ther," he smiles, seemingly proud of his sparkling white teeth. "What'll it be, hash or grass? High grade?"

"Yes to both, I'll buy some drugs."

He glares at me harshly and says in a soft, but stern voice, "I've got no drugs."

"What's all this then?" I ask pointing at the huge blocks of hash on the table.

"These aren't no drugs bro-ther," his words are no longer harsh as he has realised my ignorance. "This is hash, or pot or grass, whatever you like, ganga, but whatever it is, it is most definitely not drugs."

"From where I come from it's all drugs."

"So you're led to believe, but believe me bro-ther, it ain't all the same here in Christiania. Before there really were drugs in here, lots of nasty junk, and it was no place you wanted to be. The police would tell all the junkies to go to Christiania and that they wouldn't be arrested if they came to do their drugs here. The city's drug problem was dumped on Christiania and so we became known for it. The mothers, god bless them, they kicked those junky bums and their fucking drugs out of here. Man, I tell you, never get on the bad side of no mother! Can you believe that? A bunch of mothers kicking out the junkies, good job they did too, fucking junkies shitting and dying all over the place as our kids stepped over them. No drugs in Christiania bro-ther. We're a clean and honest people in this country. So what'll it be, ganga or hashish?"

"Minimum hash," I say while digging about my pocket for coins. I don't find many.

John's face scrunches up as though the word, 'minimum', is like fresh dog shit ground into the soul of his shoe. "Okay," he says straining to hide his disappointment that he has spent so much time talking to a punter who only wants a minimum sale. He then snaps the corner off of a honey coloured block of hash. "Don't heat this," he advises me. "It's good enough quality not to burn, just hold it in the palm of your hand for a minute and then it will crumble. I've seen you 'round a few times, you staying?"

So he does recognise me then. "I guess I am. Never meant to, but I guess I am. I was just passing through really."

"Oh man, I'm still just passing through sixteen years on!" John laughs, tipping his head back and making his afro wobble as though it is about to topple off of his head altogether. "Ninety kroner," he says, still laughing and grinning like a jester.

Next to John's stall is the Sunshine Bakery. It has a wooden step-up porch where a service window is open twenty four seven. I've never seen the window closed or the light switched off. Even when everything else in Christiania is shut down, when all the city folk have gone home and the late night drinkers are hooting and hollering in the Woodstocks bar, the Sunshine Bakery will still be open. I sit on its porch with my feet on the dirt that is Pusher Street and roll the hash into a joint. John continues his catcalling, pulling in more customers than any other with his superb salesmanship. He's positioned in the second line of pushers, which is an excellent spot and I wonder how he got there. All the other pushes at this end of the street are gruff and hard, sporting muscular, vicious dogs, having won their positions through sheer terror. I can't imagine John using this technique, although he does have a formidable size and presence to him and quite capable of ruling by the fist I'm sure, but it just doesn't seem his style.

Opposite the bakery is a small hole-in-the-wall café called Operaaen. It is dark and poky with only a few tables on the ground floor, where people sit hunched smoking and sipping coffee from glasses. They sit close together exchanging intimate conversation. A dark, crumbling stairway is on one side of the room and each step has an indentation where three hundred years of ascending feet have worn away the wood. Live jazz wafts out from above and into the night from an open window. A sax's squawk flits chaotically around a scale playing loud then soft through a single breath. The joint between my fingers is almost gone, but its affect allows me to forget music, forget jazz, the sax, loud and soft, and simply listen to the sounds as they come out, rich and vibrant. A couple of Greenlanders shuffle about to the music in a dark alcove beside Operaaen.

Further down Pusher Street, away from the city, the pushers become more approachable. A series of tables are occupied by a number of women, their giant advertisements thrust forth from chests with tight shirts. Tall, blonde, big-breasted women do an excellent trade in hash. To the right Pusher Street opens up into a quadrangle about six metres on each side. A dilapidated old building, known as the kitchen, is at the far end. I keep walking towards the gravel square past the Woodstocks bar and on to Nemoland where I buy a beer and sit by a fire that burns in a big metal barrel.

"Do na fookin push ma ya piece of shite!" I hear a familiar Scottish accent yell from over near the path that runs past Woodstocks. "Ya fookin toch ma agin an' I'll fookin' kal ya."

And there he is, Gregg the mad Scotsman, walking backwards defiantly before three men who give him an occasional light shove to help him on his way towards Pusher Street. They appear to be escorting him, staying close, but always behind so Gregg's movement can only be in the one direction. They are obviously angry with him, but not out of control. Not so for Gregg however, his face is flustered with the bright red sheen of boiling anger. Every few steps he turns and hurls abuse at the men, spittle arching from his lips and violently pointing his finger at them, "Ya fookin cants."

The men ignore his protests and threats and continue to sternly herd him towards Pusher Street. People who are drinking out the front of Nemoland notice the fracas and stand to get a better view of what is happing. "Hey, no violence!" shouts a lady from just behind me as one of the men behind Gregg gives him a particularly forceful shove that makes him stumble and almost fall to the ground.

After giving Gregg another shove forward one of the men shouts out to the lady, "He's a thief, we caught him stealing."

"More than once!" shouts another of the men from behind Gregg and gives Gregg another shove to keep him moving.

The watching crowd grows and follows the three men with Gregg bouncing between their shoves all the way down Pusher Street to the main gate of Christiania. "Don't come back!" yells one of his escorts as he gives Gregg a final shove that sends him out into the city. I recall the Bob Dylan lyrics recited to me when I first arrived in Christiania, to live outside the law you must be honest.

BATH HOUSE

Once again I wake on the chilled concrete floor of the Clubhouse. Neils has gone off to jail and I imagine him sitting on a log in the woods carving away. I smile at the thought. Then I remember last night's promise to myself to wash and I recall the pathetic drizzle of icy water from the tap in the filthy clubhouse bathroom. The thought makes me recoil deeper into my bag to hide. In time I gather enough courage to rise and stand naked, but for a pair of boxer shorts, in the morning's chill. I wonder if it's really worth it as already I have goosebumps on shivering skin.

"You do know there is a bath house in Christiania, don't you?" shouts Gunner from a table on the other side of the room where he's rolling a joint. "You look like a lemming about to jump off of a cliff!"

"I feel like one!"

Thanks to Gunner I obtain directions to the bathhouse which ends up being the big brown building opposite the Monsters restaurant, behind the Moonfisher cafe. Walking into the bathhouse my chill is immediately eaten by a blast of hot air and I am confronted by a changing area with people in various states of undress. Two young guys sit behind a counter. One prepares a joint while the other takes fifteen kroner off of me as the entrance fee and towel hire. I undress in the changing area, hanging my clothes on hooks that skirt the wall, feeling self-conscious and awkward.

From the changing area I scamper down a wide corridor lined with a single, long wash basin above which is a narrow mirror running the entire length of the wall. A toilet occupies the first cubical on the far wall and another five cubicles sprout shower nozzles. For the first time in more than two weeks I am able to stand beneath a hot stream of prickly water and it feels amazing. I had all but forgotten what a luxury it is to have steaming jets of hot water massage the back of my head and shoulders. I stand motionless for a while smelling the gunk being washed down the drain at my feet. It's not busy in the bathhouse, just a couple of guys and girls enjoying the steaming pleasures. I turn to face the wall when the girls walk by my shower cubicle.

Opposite the cubicles is a wooden door to a sauna. It has a window, but condensation hinders vision inside. Opening the door I feel a rush of warm air and am faced with a blinding wall of steam. An irritated voice shouts. "Close the door!"

I step through the wall of steam and close the door as quickly as possible. Wooden benches, three levels high, line the sauna's walls, and a mud smeared woman lies on the tiled floor. Her legs stretch up and over her body as she makes good effort to touch her toes on the floor behind her head. She's naked, of course, and in this position her shiny, round buttocks are pointed directly at me with her flower blossoming in between. She slowly recoils her legs to the floor and sits up to stretch her arms behind her head. I manage to step past the woman and sit on a bench without it appearing too obvious that the sight of a naked woman isn't an everyday occurrence for me.

Directly across is a guy in his thirties. Next to him is a small woman with close cropped snow-blond hair and defined shoulder muscles. And next to her another woman rests back against the sauna wall as she rubs mud over an arm. A tattoo of a dragon runs up the side of her body, its tail disappearing under a round breast. Realising that I am taking too much notice where the tattoo disappears I divert my gaze down to the mud smeared woman practising yoga on the floor. She stands to smear mud over her buttocks.

My heart pounds and I tap a beat on the bench with my fingers as I think about the consequences of the erection that currently stirs my loins.

"Hi, hi," says the guy opposite me, a thankful distraction. He smiles as though he can sense my unease. "You know, it is a good place to have a sauna, yes?"

It's all I can do to smile back at him, willing my eyes away from the women and taking deep breathes, attempting to regain calm. "My name is Nico." he says. "I come from the city most days to use Christiania's Bathhouse as my apartment doesn't have a proper a bathroom."

It's enough to suppress my rising desires and I am able to relax into the sauna's heat. Nico's eyes are a deep, almost bottomless blue and he possesses a piercing gaze as though he is trying to look deep into me. He leans back against the wall as sweat beads high on his forehead and follows the crooked line of his nose, dripping off to splash against his chest. With Nico talking I am able to ignore the sweating, muddied skin and tight curves of the naked female bodies around us. There is a small metal dish half full of mud that has been left on the seat beside me. I dip my fingers into its stickiness and smear mud across my chest, down my arms and over my thighs. Sweat mixes with it to create a gooey film that covers my skin.

Nico's insists that I follow him as he exits the sauna to stand by an open window to allow a cool breeze to harden the mud until it forms a thin crust over our bodies. Each time I move an arm or leg I can feel the crust break and crack. Once the mud has totally dried we wash off in icy cold showers leaving my skin crisp, clean and silky smooth. While drying off and getting dressed in the changing area, Nico suggests that we go to smoke a joint at the Moonfisher café.

It is only a short walk to the Moonfisher, just around the corner where we find a small crowd sitting on a long bench running down half the length of the building's front. Others form a small queue at the entrance waiting for a man to carry out a tray of glasses. A small rock wall cuts a semicircle across the gravelled area beyond which is a small park that shines a brilliant green glow in the sunlight. Nico and I wait while the bottleneck into the Moonfisher clears and shuffle inside.

A long service counter runs down the right hand side of the Moonfisher, with a glass case displaying a long row of teas above platters of pastries and sandwiches. We order tea and Nico leads us away from the serving area and into the vast cavernous room. About a quarter of the room is built up, like a stage, four feet off of the ground. Two pool tables are on each of the café's split levels and the rest of the area is taken up by scattered black tables and chairs. Huge arched windows run around the space allowing so much light into the room that I feel as though we have just entered a small cathedral. Two-thirds up each window, where the arches begin, a row of pot plants runs a line of green foliage around the whole room. It's noisy with chattering conversations, smacking billiard balls and reggae dub playing out through giant cube speakers perched high in the corners.

Nico leads me to a table on the raised level running across the back wall of the cafe. An old couple with silver hair and woollen cardigans chat at a table next to us. The man prepares a chillum and a dog lazes at his feet snoozing in the amplified sun.

Nico places a small round piece of leather on the table next to his steaming tea. He crumbles hash on to the leather and roasts a cigarette to extract the nicotine before producing a highly polished mamut with a gold ring inlaid around the centre of its length. He is so exact in gluing the joint together that a ridge of paper is left sticking out from it. He sets this on fire with a quick flick of his lighter and holds the joint up as the excess paper burns off. Proud of his achievement he holds it out to me, stares deep into my eyes and says, "Light it up, if we can share a sauna we can share other things too."

As I take the joint from Nico, our hands brush against each other a little more than I intended them to. I spark the joint and inhale deeply, holding my breath for a few seconds, tilt my head back and blow a great waft of smoke up into the Moonfisher's ceiling.

"Great joint," I say. "A freaking masterpiece actually."

The joint, including the mamut, is close to twenty centimetres long and with the quantity of hash that it contains I am beginning to wonder how the two of us will manage to get through it and what state we might be in if we do. I pass the joint back to Nico who takes an almighty toke and blows the smoke directly at me, once again looking deep into my eyes. The joint travels back and forth between us until it is smoked down to the mamut. The regga dub seems to thump slower and the cracking of the billiard balls appears to be more distant, but the gap between me and Nico has grown smaller. He's leaning over towards me and touching my arm as he speaks. And it hits me, Nico is gay! I sit back, stunned that I hadn't realised he was gay earlier. With all those looks, sweating naked in the sauna, it was obvious. You don't go having a cup of tea with a stranger you've just met, naked, in a sauna, unless you're gay. Therefore, I conclude, Nico must think I'm also gay, why else would I be here? We're on a date!

"Thanks for the joint Nico," I say with a smile as I am more amused by my predicament than confronted by it.

Nico senses the change in me and rests his hand on my forearm. "Must you go, so soon?"

COSMIC FLOWER

After more than a week sleeping on the cold, hard concrete floor of the clubhouse I am moving to Lonni's attic in the big old solid barn on the far side of the lake. It is with much appreciation that I say thanks to Poo, Gunner and Jacob and make my way down through Christiania across the lake and into the area known as Dussen. On the way I pass the home made from a red railway container. The old guy with crazy hair is twisting some wire around a pole out the front. He glances at me and notices my backpack then looks again at my face, taking careful notice as though he is recording me in his memory.

At the Kosmic Bloomst, Lonni explains that she sleeps up in her attic while her two girls, Nin and Franny share a huge double bed downstairs next to a kitchen area. There is a spare mattress for me up in the attic on which Lonni has laid out a clean, crisp sheet. The attic is dusty, but could not be described as dirty. It is rustic and inviting. Above our mattresses the walls converge to form a roof that mimics the letter "A". Huge horizontal beams slice through the space with peeling splinters the size of a pencil. The floorboards are great monster lumber of varying widths laid down unevenly, so there are large gaps between some and I can spy through the floor to see Lonni making coffee in the kitchen below. Four small windows are framed in the attic's roof and out of each I can see the green foliage of trees illuminated by the last rays of sunlight. Birds are chirping and footsteps scrunch on the gravelled path outside as someone walks by. Toys and games are spread all over the attic floor.

With two cups of coffee in hand Lonni ascends the curved stairway to the attic, having put Nin and Franny to bed. She has just come back from a parent teacher interview at the girls' school and she appears somewhat flustered by the experience. "I'm sooo confused," she says with a long sigh to follow.

I slosh my coffee around in its mug aware that I am a guest, a tourist, in her house, and not wanting to pry into Lonni's personal affairs.

"This place is getting me down," she says, her face is long and sad. She looks exhausted. "I really think it's time that I moved back to the city, get away from here." She throws out her arm in a motion intended to wipe all of Christiania and her problems away.

"How could you want to leave this place?" I can't fathom what she's saying. "It's fantastic, amazing."

"This place...," she pauses, searching her emotions and attempting to translate them into words, "....is many different things to different people and now I just want something normal. You know, a straight life." Her hand comes shooting out from her forehead to emphasise the significance of the straight life.

"I have two girls living in this barn with no bathroom, that's crazy. To go to the toilet they have to walk down the road to an outhouse. How can I bring girls up like that when all their friends live in the city. I am craaaaazy!" Lonni reaches out to punch my arm while leaning backwards and giggling, "I'm craaaaazy!"

It is one of the things that I am starting to love about Lonni. She is facing some really hard challenges, but she still always manages to make light of her situation and laugh regardless of the obvious pain she feels.

"My son is straight you know, he's older, twenty, and he lives with his father in the city."

"Do you see him much?"

"No, not much, but I'm seeing him next weekend."

"What about his father?"

"No, our time together is over. We had lots of fun for a while. He treated me like a princess. Or sometimes like a fairy, depending on how he felt. He's straight now too, like my son. Not when we were together though. He was as far from being straight as anyone could get. Back then we went all over the place, to a different country every day. Oh, we had this huge beautiful candy apple red Jaguar that would just drive and drive and drive. We'd spend whole weeks in that car driving down to Afghanistan to get hashish to bring back to Denmark."

"Just you and him?"

"No, there were three of us, we had so much fun. My girlfriend from the city was with us as well. It was such a laugh, coming back from the East with a red Jaguar full of hashish, all the way we'd be nervous and scared but always laughing at each other, it was so much fun. Then when we'd get back to the city we'd have so much money to spend all over town, the best restaurants the best hotels and wine. And then when we met our guru, he was ours together, we were so in love. Life was so good then, all the time going from one country to the next following our guru. England one week, Italy the next then off to America, global jet setting spiritualists I guess. So much fun and sooo fuuunny!"

I love listening to Lonni. The way she speaks is so expressive and her grin is huge with flashing white teeth, it can only make me smile and laugh also.

"Our Guru. He was wonderful, just thinking of him makes me feel warm. We met him after having just come back from the East. We followed him for a long time, all over, from England to America and India. It was so wonderful. In the end he told us the *The Knowledge* then insisted that we stop following him. Now he lives on Malibu beach in California. I feel so happy now just talking about it and remembering,"

"The knowledge, about what?"

"I can't tell you."

"Go on, tell me."

"I can't"

"Why not?"

"I'm not allowed to, but I know someone who can, maybe I'll ask him."

We continue talking into the early hours of the morning and deep into a bottle of whiskey and I never consciously make a decision to go to sleep.

WORK FOR FOOD

It is another beautiful spring day and I'm lucky to simply drift around town, something I have become expert at over the past few days. I usually stop halfway over the wooden bridge to view the many church towers of Copenhagen poking their spires above Christiania's wall of green trees, smiling to myself as it conjures an image of children stretching onto their toes to see over the wall of a forbidden garden. Village folk rattle past over the wooden planks on their oddly configured bicycles calling out, "Hi hi," as they trundle past. There are many and varied bicycles that are peddled around Christiania. My favorites have rear wheels and seats just like any bicycle, but the front is elongated with a flat carry space down low. Riders use them to cart things around, usually crates of beer, but I've seen some with big armchairs positioned out front in front of the rider so the person they are carrying sits in a comfy armchair just as they might sit at home in their loungeroom. Other bikes have a big wooden box supported by an axle and two wheels out the front of what is otherwise a normal bike. The children's playschool has one of these and I often see it being peddled around town with four or five little kids poking their heads out of the box out in front, smiling as their hair is blown about in the wind. Another guy that I've seen riding around has a horizontal metal bar that stretches from the front of his bike projecting his front wheel out about eight feet. Atop the metal bar is a snowboard and when he gets enough speed up, he jumps across his handlebars to ride the snowboard while the spinning centrifugal forces keep the whole bike upright. I have seen him a few times surfing along the road, arms stretched out from his sides for balance.

Approaching Inkoopen, Christiania's general store, the population of dogs dramatically increases. All shapes and sizes, Great Danes, big hounds and tiny squirrel dogs that are consistently more trouble than the bigger dogs. It is around Inkoopen that the buildings cease being elaborately constructed works of architectural art and are replaced by the old military buildings that the Christianites have occupied. This part of town is more densely populated and the social action thickens. The bathhouse and the Moonfisher are near Inkoopen, as is Monsters restaurant.

"Hi, hi!," says Christof, smiling as he extends his arm to shake my hand.

"Christof. It's good to receive such a welcome."

"Are you here to work?"

"Is it lunch time?" I reply.

"Just been," smiles back Christof. "We had a busy lunch and have plenty of dishes. I say you do those dishes over there and we feed you a late lunch. Yes?" His voice booms and he is hard to refuse.

So I find myself slopping my hands around in a deep sink with a not too high pile of dirty dishes by my side. Behind me Christof continues to flop his rag around cleaning the tables as he dances around to a slow jazz tune that plays on the stereo. After a while I noticed Carlos smoking at the back of the restaurant, just a silhouette and a wisp of white smoke. He notices me watching him and tips his joint as a salute. The smells coming from the Monsters kitchen are scrumptious and I'm wondering what to ask for lunch. However, Christof keeps putting tray after tray of food away leaving my choice of lunch to less and less. Before I can say anything to Christof about the dwindling food options in walks a black guy with dreadlocks. "Hey, yaaaaa'll," he says with a big cheesy smile, in an accent that could only be American.

"Hi, hi," greats Christof and shakes the guy's hand.

"Earth," he says to me. Maybe it's the flashing smile, I don't know, but straight away I like the guy.

"Where's that bad man Carlos?" demands Earth.

Carlos speaks up from the back of the room. "Did you bring my 'erbs?" he asks, mocking the French language.

"Twenty different herbs, direct from China and straight to you."

"What are they for?" I ask.

Earth frowns, deepening the wrinkles already set into his face. "Cooking, of course."

"But not for Monster's," interrupts Carlos. "For me. They're medicinal."

"Take care of ulcers, deficiencies, make you live longer," continues Earth. "All-round good stuff. Do you want some?"

"You selling?" I state the obvious.

"You bet he is," adds Carlos handing Earth a hundred Kroner note. "Don't let old Earth fool you, nothing's for free."

"I dunno, he seems like a nice guy," I say smiling at Earth.

"A nice guy! Sheeeeit, a nice guy. I've come all the way from ol' US of A to Christiania and spent two years among all this just to be called a nice guy. Sheeeeeit." He's still smiling though.

"I'm a terrible guy," laughs Earth.

"The worst, a bad guy in a nice guys disguise," says Carlos.

"There's lots of those," adds Christof, obviously the sensitive giant who has been hurt once too often.

"Yes, let me give you some advice," says Carlos to me, serious now. "In Christiania many people will be nice to your face, but building alliances behind your back. You see, if things ever get really heavy here for you you can survive only if people speak out for you. The only way you can get kicked out is if there is a significant alliance against you. It is always the person who's nicest to you that turns out to be plotting an alliance against you."

Just as Carlos ends his advice, Earth turns to me with a gleaming smile and says, "Yeah, man, I've been here two years and one day I thought I was badass enough to go sit up on Pusher Street and sell some skunk that I'd grown, but straight away I had all the pushers yelling at me and they kicked me out of Pusher Street. Now I've got all those pushers pissed at me and it is kinda unnerving to tell you the truth."

We all laugh at the way Earth says this. It is bad news that he's telling, but the whole time he is smiling and laughing himself. Carlos hands around his joint and Earth sits down to talk with him. The jazz is turned up and I enjoy a thick, warm slice of bread, a bowl of cauliflower and leek soup with seaweed salad on the side. Just as Earth is leaving, after a long talk with Carlos, he leans down to me at the table where I slurp soup and whispers, "Christiania is a small place, make only friends." He smiles and walks out the door.

THE MOONFISHER

Each Monday the collective that runs the Moonfisher close the café and clean. Poo, from the W.C. Fields Club, has arranged for me to clean with them. Hopefully to get paid, but he didn't say anything about that. While I've spent a considerable amount of time at the Moonfisher drinking tea and smoking I don't actually know anyone there, so I fidget nervously as I knock on the locked door.

A female face appears behind the glass and mouths something to me. I presume that she is speaking Danish as I have no idea what she is trying to tell me. After a moment when she realises my incomprehension and mouths again in silent English, over-enunciating the words, "We are closed."

"Poo sent me, he told me to ask for Lunar," I shout through the glass.

Footsteps reverberate from behind the door. "Hi Hi," says a woman with a stern smile. "Are you Poo's friend?"

"Yes, you're Luna?"

She grabs my arm. "Quick, come in before anyone sees the door open. We're closed this morning."

Having dragged me inside Lunar hands me a cloth and shows me through to the large open kitchen area, with a long wide stainless steel bench top and sink with piles and piles of pots and pans on a shelf below. "This is the job, the bench the sink the tiles, the stove, the oven and the fat fan up above." Lunar then leaves me to it.

A huge arched window is right by the kitchen and the sun is streaming in, making all the steal glisten. When I fill the sink with soapsuds they sparkle with all the colours of the rainbow. The kitchen is in a back room, behind the serving area and a set of stairs lead up to a small loft where a young man in a turtleneck sweater sits at a desk. An archway leads into the serving area and the cafe floor beyond. I can see members of the Moonfisher collective cleaning as they jive around to funk music. Around twenty people are sweeping and mopping, wiping and scrubbing, bopping away to some great tunes. Many of them I have seen around the Moonfisher before, serving tea, clearing tables or playing pool. They nod and smile to me before I return to scrubbing the tiles, cooktop and every other inanimate object within the vicinity of the kitchen. Later, one of the Moonfisher's crew walks into the kitchen and hands me a freshly packed stone chillum. As he passes it to me his eyes sparkle friendship under wire-framed glasses. I create an airtight seal between my pinkie and ring fingers cup my hand to my mouth and hold the chillum vertical. He strikes a match and holds it to the mouth of the chillum while I puff a couple of times at the other end drawing the flame down. After each puff a flame shoots out from the chillum followed by great billowing clouds of smoke. I cough and splutter as Lunar arrives and says, "Okay, we start cooking lunch, yes."

The chillum is taken away by the guy who brought it and he asks something of Lunar in Danish, listens to her response, grunts and nods, then leaves the kitchen. Lunar glances at me while rolling her sleeves up to wash her hands. "So you make some pasta in boiling water and I make a sauce and you help with a big salad." Then she grunts as though to emphasise the instructions.

I snap to it and grab the biggest pot in the kitchen and haul it to the sink as Lunar swivels the tap head across to start filling it up. We work like this, as a team, making lunch quickly. Soon we have a big bowl of pasta ready, carrying it out on serving dishes to a large table created, like a jigsaw, from all of the cafes' small tables. As we are setting the food down on the table Lunar says to me, "Normally we wouldn't let you stay for lunch as you are not a part of the Moonfisher collective, but seeing you don't understand Danish you can stay. You can't eat lunch at the big table though. You must sit over there, by the window."

I'm just glad I get to eat lunch. So I take a plate and pile it with pasta, salad and chunks of bread and go sit at the one small table left, way in the back of the room, under a huge arched window through which I can see the dogs crapping on the grass in the park outside. I eat my lunch and pretend not to observe the meeting. While I don't understand what people are saying it is easy to get a sense of the meeting as it unfolds. As the Moonfisher collective munches through a big lunch, the man who I had seen working in the office above the kitchen, Frank, I hear him being called, sits at one end of the table and reads short statements from a piece of paper. After each statement various collective members add comments, interject and argue with each other. Lunar speaks infrequently, but when she does it is forcefully and hers is often the last word to be said on a matter before the silence of agreement settles and Frank surveys the collective, seeking confirmation, before moving on. With each point he takes the time for each collective member to have a chance to be heard. Many in the collective choose not to say anything at all, most interject only on single points, while a few need to have their say on each one. In the arguing of some points voices are raised and once Lunar has to shout a bit louder than everyone else to calm things down. As the last piece of bread is wiped across a plate and blocks of hash are brought out onto the table many things seem to have been decided. Frank has been able to work through his list effectively and everyone seems relaxed. Lunar speaks my name among a slow, ambling passage in Danish. She looks over to me, followed by the gaze of the rest of the collective. Following a moment's pause of silence, Frank says, "Yes"

From around the table a slow chorus of, "Yes," follows.

Frank continues in English. "We've just decided that if you want some more work you can help Axel build the fence around the park outside. We have decided to build a fence to stop the dogs shitting on the grass."

I manage to stammer, "Yeah, that would be great."

"Good," says a small man with a high forehead and long black hair that drops around his ears in wild curls. "We'll sort things out later."

With that the Moonfisher crew start to break up the meeting and arrange the chairs and tables again ready for the re-opening of the café. I help Lunar and a few others clear the plates from the table and do the dishes.

RUNESTONE

I am basking in the sun out front of the Moonfisher. The day is perfect, blue sky and a shining sun. Earth arrives with a friend from Sweden and they sit down to join me in the sun and together we talk the afternoon away. Axel, who is building the fence around this park for the Moonfisher, turns up with a couple of other people. They congregate around a large white stone that sits in the middle of the Moonfisher's park. Axel introduces me to one of the men with him. Erik, a self proclaimed Viking, comes from Gotenberg in Sweden, but strongly insists it is not a place where traditional Swedish culture resides. He says bluntly that he is embarrassed to be Swedish, preferring to emphasise that his home village in Sweden historically derives from Danish ancestry. "We are a completely different people to the Swedes," he claims, keen for me to understand that he is not Swedish.

Erik is carving an inscription into the stone that sits prominently in the Moonfisher's park. "Usually I make silver jewelry," he tells me. "But one day I was in the Moonfisher and they asked me if I'd carve a dragon on one side of this stone and a poem on the other. I thought it would take only three weeks, but now I think it will take much longer."

"It's more than just a stone," chimes in Axel. "Erik is being humble. It is actually the first runestone to be laid in over a thousand years."

"A couple of days later a bloody great stone was sitting out the front of the Moonfisher and I was told to go to work on it," says Eirk, "So far I've been here, on and off, for two weeks and I've so much left to do."

"So what's wrong with it, why's it ruined?"

Eric and Axel aren't sure if I'm joking.

"Really, what is a runestone?" I ask

Eric fills me in. "In the old days, a thousand years ago, Vikings would erect runestones to commemorate things, people mostly and sometimes events. Like when a Viking warrior died they might lay a runestone to tell the tale of his life; or after a great battle Vikings might lay a runestone to commemorate it. The ruen itself is the old Viking alphabet. I am carving this one just like the old ones. On the back here I am carving a big dragon and on the front I will carve a poem that old Palle has written. Do you know Palle?"

I shake my head no.

"Palle is a well known poet in Christiania. I don't know the poem word for word yet, but basically it talks about when Catholicism found its way north, through the Roman Empire, the end of the world became upon itself. The old thinking, the old Viking ways, were gone, driven out of people's lives. Mythology says that all the Viking gods went to war and a wolf, known as Skoll, ate the Sun Goddess, Sol. Destruction of the Viking world as it had previously existed was upon us, but before the old Viking gods were defeated and devoured by Skoll, the Sun Goddess, while she was dying, gave birth to a daughter, Sunna. The poem, Palle's poem, that I'm carving on the stone talks of waiting for the daughter of the sun Goddess to return from exile and bring the old Viking ways back."

"And by placing and carving this runestone here in Christiania it will give her a place to return to," Axel concludes.

Erik lifts his head in thought. "Actually, I think just by carving and placing the runestone she has already returned. "He smiles a great big blissful smile. "I like it, as by carving this stone and placing it here it really is, in a way, the return of the old Viking ways."

It is easy to see that Erik loves his work. I've seen him during the past few weeks sitting on a little stool working his tools to create a sacred stone. "I just love it," he says. "Not just the work, but the stone itself, like I am falling in love with the bloody thing. As I'm carving I keep thinking of the stone and the song, I think it is a Stranglers song, about a man with his camel in the desert and how he falls in love with the camel that has no name. I kind of feel that way about the stone."

Somehow he makes a weird sort of sense that I can almost understand. "I feel like I am creating something historical," says Erik, staring at his stone with what can only be love in his eyes.

After a while Axel remembers that there is a party in Christiania tonight, so we make our way down past Monsters restaurant towards the village wall to Detlif's home. Axel explains that it is Detlif's birthday and as we arrive we are confronted by what appears to be a whole cow rotating slowly over a fire. Three kegs of beer are lined up next to a tap and the smoke from joints and chillums is thick in the early evening air. Detlif's garden is small, but crowded, and my senses are pricked with the proximity of many beautiful girls. Already one is staring intently at me. I am only able to glance at her intermittently due to the intensity of her gaze. She is tall and blond, like so many of the Danish women, but while many of the Danes are solidly built this woman is slender yet toned in muscle. Her face is finely carved and her posture is straight and confident. While we continue to meet each other's gaze throughout the evening she keeps her distance from me and I understand why when Erik, the Viking, puts his arms around her and cuddles her.

The night grows darker. The roasting cow diminishes to the reveller's appetite and the beer kegs empty. Everyone is getting very drunk when Detlif produces a chainsaw. "That fucking tree!" he is yelling. "I don't like it. It is always in the way!" he screams, smiling all the while.

"Kill the tree!" starts a chant amongst many of his friends. "Kill the tree!"

The chainsaw growls as Detlif revs it, Grrrrrrrrrr, grrrrrrrrr! With the party cheering him on he stumbles over to the tree and cuts it down. It's not a huge tree, but as it is snapped by its own weight it groans loudly, splinters and begins to tilt towards his house. The party screams, through its laughter, and revellers dash in all directions to escape the falling tree.

Thump, swoosh. Crunch.

Silence.

The party breaks out into huge fits of laughter as the tree finally comes to rest leaning on Detlif's roof. People are falling over chairs, each other and the tree as they attempt to contain their laughter. A huge cheer issues forth and Detlif raises the revving chainsaw above his head cackling with manic laughter.

The felling of the tree sets off stage two of the party. Most parties have a stage two; stage one being moderate drinking, polite conversation and awkward mingling. Stage two being drunken, out of control, wild revelling. I've always thought that in order for a real party to occur three things need happen. First, there needs to be a fight, then a relationship break up and finally someone has to throw up.

"Who cut down the tree?" yells an angry voice from somewhere close by in the darkness. "Who cut down the tree?" It quickly repeats, demanding a response.

A relative silence engulfs the party broken only by occasional giggles and the sounds of people tripping and falling. Detlif walks forward to the front of his yard and is illuminated by the fire that roasts the half-eaten cow. "It was my tree and it had to go!" he states drunkenly to an old man who has emerged into the firelight from the darkness.

"You can't just go chopping trees down!"

"I just did!"

"But you can't!"

The man is enraged. "The meeting will hear about this."

"The meeting!" screams Detlif and, in jest, leans over to grab the chainsaw.

"Yes, I will tell people. People will see it for themselves in the morning." The man, dressed in a long night robe, shuffles his feet back over to a brightly colored gypsy wagon complete with huge wagon wheels.

While no-one was punched or pushed I am still happy to tick it off as a fight and feel satisfied that we are truly on the way to having a real party.

Having become quite drunk I find myself constantly tripping over things in Detlif's poorly lit front yard. I therefore determine it best to sit down on a large log near a small fire burning away from the party's epicenter. Next to me on the log sit two women, one dark and sultry and the other slim with long blond hair and fair skin. The darker one introduces herself as Maria and starts passing me very strong whisky and cokes in small plastic cups. While she has a beauty to her it is her friend, the blonde, who attracts my interest. I am, however, becoming way too drunk and my words slur encouraging me to say less rather than more. The blonde, who has been introduced to me as Aneka, takes little interest in my presence. Maria hands me more whisky and cokes.

Erik's girlfriend, who I shared many a wanting gaze with earlier on in the evening, is in private, yet intense, conversation with Erik. It isn't a calm conversation and appears to be developing into an argument. Both of them seem to be becoming more and more emotional until the blonde stands up, unlatches a chain from around her neck and throws it at Erik. Erik appears bemused and then becomes more than a little angry and he too stands, yelling at the woman. The argument has quickly become a fight and many of the revellers focus their attention on what is obviously a relationship break up. Erik's girlfriend storms away from the party and disappears into the night's darkness.

Relationship break-up, check, almost a real party!

As Maria hands me another whisky and coke I am scanning through all the revellers to see if anyone is looking seedy enough to complete the final requirement of a real party. I would much prefer it came from her friend Aneka, but a free whisky and coke is a free whisky and coke and Maria has a very happy, welcoming way about her. Her friend Aneka still pays me no attention at all. I'm chatting with Maria, so drunk that I'm unsure exactly what is coming out of my mouth, gulping the whisky in big swigs, spilling it down my front, then falling off of the back of the log. I lay on my back staring up at the stars. The fire pleasantly warms my legs as my body begins a slow, wave like spinning that usually proceeds… "Oh, god," I moan as I drag myself a few metres away from the fire and two beautiful women before finally rolling on my side and puking into a bush. I lay there prone until the spinning stops. "Yep," I think to myself through a drunken mind fog. "A real party!"

FENCE POLITICS

While waiting for Axel I sizzle bacon in the Moonfisher's kitchen and crack eggs into a fry pan. Beautiful sunrays stream through the giant arched window that occupies the entire wall in the kitchen. I only have to pay half-price for the bacon and eggs, if I cook them myself, as I am building their fence. The Moonfisher crew working this morning are taking things very slow as it is too early for many customers to venture in.

After about an hour and a half of breakfast and joint smoking Axel finally arrives and we start to work on the fence. His six-month-old daughter is with him and she is left parked happy in her pram as Axel proceeds to tell me about the job at hand. The Moonfisher collective have decided to clean up some unused land and create a park around the runestone that Erik is carving. "They need a fence," Axel tells me. "Because all the dogs in Christiania seem to love shitting on this grass."

The fence is already in construction with four thick posts sticking out of the ground around the park's perimeter. A fifth post lies on the ground.

"Bloody hell!" despairs Axel. "The fence has been broken! This happens every day. This place, Chrisitania, is so frustrating. We're building this fence to keep the dogs from shitting on the grass, but people keep breaking it down."

From the path that runs between the Moonfisher Café and the Green Hall comes an old man, beer in hand, and he says to Axel, "There are already too many fences in Christiania, too many divides. How can the Free Town be free when there are fences dividing this from that?"

"But we're trying to keep the dogs from shitting on the grass!" explains Axel, with more than a little exasperation in his voice.

"No, no no," says the man. "Too many divides, and besides, the dogs are wild, you'll never stop them!"

"I will if I build the bloody fence and people stop kicking the posts down!"

Watching Axel and the man gradually enter into an argument about the validity of a new fence in Christiania I begin to understand the nature of living in a community without rules or any kind of authority. As I have witnessed many times here, the argument rules supreme, the argument is the authority. There are no police or courthouses, no real governing councils making decisions that people must adhere to, just the rule of the argument. The high court of argument, the supreme argument; won by an appeal of argument!

Having seen such an argument occurring a couple of the Moonfisher collective come out to the grassed area and join in. Lunar is present and as far as arguments go she is a bit of a presiding judge. She weighs in and shouts and gestures with her hands until the man on the other side of the fence throws up his hands in despair and walks off supping his beer. The fence building continues and we do our best to build it strong.

THE TAXMUM

Today is a part of a long weekend, I am told, and with the long weekend come the Swedes. It seems that half the population of Malmo, just over the narrow strait of water in Sweden, has decided to unwind with a visit to Christiania. Hundreds, thousands of them are roaming the village, all up and down Pusher Street, all over Dussen and South Dussen where the Kosmic Bloomst sits among the trees by the lake. The Swedes have come to party. Already, before the sun has passed its apex, they are swilling beer and singing like football hooligans. A stark contrast to the sedate social drunkenness generally witnessed within Christiania with the standard set by the solemn, quite Greenlanders who shuffle about in the dark within the alcoves of Pusher Street. If the drunks of Christiania do yell and shout it is generally part of an important political discussion or governance issue on a topic which directly affects their day-to-day life. A couple of drunken Swedes rip off their shirts and dive hooting and hollering into the lake across from the Kosmic Bloomst. They are the first people I have seen who have dared immerse themselves in that lake. Sure it looks naturally clean, but I just can't forget that it is smack in the middle of a thousand-year-old city and only God knows what it contains.

Christiania is staging a football carnival on the Meadow of Peace, a large grassed area to the side of Nemoland. It seems that most of the village is involved. From a grassy knoll I can see Jacob and Gunner from the W.C. Fields Club playing in the current game. The rest of the old W.C. Field's punks are hooting and hollering on the far end of the sideline, beers in hand and a giant hash pipe carved out of a huge pumpkin. Sadly Neils is not among them so I say a quick prayer for him out the forest prison, hoping he is enjoying some peaceful wood carving.

The team that the old punks are playing is entirely made up of young women dressed in catsuits, hooded red leotards with long, stiff tails and plastic cat ears protruding from the top of their heads. Whiskers and black noses are painted on their faces and they are caning the old punks.

Although to be fair, Jacob from W.C. Fields team is taking it to the red cats with a sturdy tenaciousness.

He knocks one flat and she falls over backwards, turning in the air to douse her fall she lands on her front side with her face in the earth. Without mercy Jacob continues to run over her so as he can angle the ball to his right. Accelerating with long, youthful strides he slides his foot across the ball propelling it towards one of his team-mates who clumsily catches it with his foot and runs out of control over the ball. In a whirr of tails and whiskers a cat pounces and effortlessly owns the ball as she dashes off towards the centre line to cheers from fellow felines on the sideline. The old punks that are not playing curse and throw their arms about in exasperation, swigging their beers and slapping each other on the back. Along the field a whole crowd of mothers and children, dogs, drunks, rastas, pushers and Swedish tourists have gathered to watch the game.

As the sun finally sets after a long Scandinavian dusk that seems to have lasted for half the day, I sit with Poo and Gunner at a party under the half-built frame of a house down the road from Monsters. A woodbox rhythm band is playing on the far side of a large bonfire and a father and son dance wildly to the music. Both have their faces painted like clowns and wear oversized baggy pants and breeches. The boy holds onto his father's outstretched arms, leans back and walks up his chest to loop his legs over his father's wide shoulders. The boy then falls backwards so his head swings down to dangle between his father's knees. His father leans back to counter the weight and swings him back up again until the boy is sitting on his shoulder's facing backwards. They swing again and again twirling around the fire in wild circles.

Enjoying the spectacle of love between father and son and the warm glow of the bonfire, I smile and am content to listen to Poo and Gunner ramble on in Danish as they become progressively drunker. There are many women and children about, but Poo, Gunner and I sit back at the edge of the party talking and slowly sipping beers. From out of the darkness and into the firelight comes a bike that is jam-packed with more kids in its front carry box. In the box are five little kids all holding onto the side, which comes up to just bellow their chins. They are all smiling with big cheesy grins obviously happy to have arrived at the party and thrilled at their mode of transport.

"The Naver's are building this house for the children," Gunner tells me pointing to the partially constructed wooden frame. "A safe place for them to play away from the pushers and dogs." He turns his body to be able to look behind him. "Over there they build a place for animals so the children can touch and pat them."

I assume the men who are all dressed similarly to each other are the Naver's. There are six of them around the fire, all wearing wide, straight-legged velvet bellbottom pants and smart velvet waistcoats with elaborate pirate-like shirts underneath that have big frilly cuffs and collars. Velvet top hats are perched on their heads at various angles and each Naver has a full, wild beard that appears never to have been touched by the barber's trimming scissors.

"Who are the Naver's?" I ask Gunner.

"It's kind of hard to explain," he responds to me with a puzzled look on his face. "They are kind of a club like us at W.C. Fields."

Poo laughs, "Don't bullshit him, they don't drink anywhere near the amount of beer that we do!"

"I'm not," Gunner's laughing. "How would you explain them?"

Poo ponders a while with his brow furrowed and his gaze distant as he explores for a possible explanation before chuckling to Gunner. "Well, they're kind of like the W.C. Fields..."

Gunner's laughing grows stronger and Poo continues with a smile. "But they have been around a lot longer than us." He looks to Gunner for confirmation which he offers with a sweeping motion of his hand.

"They have been around for hundreds of years. More a brotherhood than a club."

Gunner is nodding with agreement.

"Perhaps two or three hundred years, maybe longer. They are all carpenters, master craftsmen, that is the thing that makes them a brotherhood I guess."

He looks up into the partially constructed wooden frame before continuing. "When they build something they don't use nails or screws. This children's house is being made entirely without metal, only wood. When they join two pieces of wood they use small joints."

"Stronger than nails," interjects Gunner as though he is an authority on building.

Poo continues, "I think that they are mostly Germans, but they travel all over the world building things. These Navers have just come back from India where they helped to build a hospital. They have already built the Banana House in Christiania, have you seen that?"

"No", I say, but I do remember an oddly shaped building that resembled a banana with grass growing over its roof.

"They've been coming to Christiania since it began, and we welcome them because of things they build, like this Children's House."

"How great would it be to grow up in Christiania?" I wonder out loud.

With the unmistakable gleam of pride in his eyes Poo responds, "See that lovely young girl over there. She is the first of Christiania's third generation. Her mother was the first to be borne here."

A beautiful young girl no more than two years old plays happily near the bike-cart that delivered the load of children. Her hair is the purist of white and hangs down in scraggly tufts to rest on her shoulders. She turns and smiles. Behind her a woman stands with the same white hair fluttering in the gentle wind.

"Money!" yells a woman sitting close by the fire. "We need more money, always money, it so spoils everything!" She is drunk, but only a little. She stands clasping the handle of a metal bucket. "We have run out of money to build the Children's House, who's coming with me?"

"Where to?" I ask as she walks past me. "Where do you get money from?"

"Follow me," she says. "You can hold the bucket."

She gives me the bucket and I follow her down past Inkopen, the Bathhouse and Woodstocks Bar. I don't know her at all so I am hesitant to ask exactly where we are going. She's outpacing me with a real purpose to her stride and her brow is furrowed in determination. I have to jog to keep up and eventually we find ourselves at the end of Pusher Street. She walks straight up to the first pusher we come to. He sits high on a stool with a small table attached to a metal pole that is concreted into the ground. At this end of Pusher Street, farthest from Christiania's main entrance, the pushers are mostly family men and too old for the macho bravado of the pushers near the main entrance. "Money for the Children's house," says the lady, grabbing the bucket I am carrying and setting it down roughly on the pusher's little table, my hand still clasped to it.

With a resigned smile the pusher takes a few notes out of his pocket and drops them in the bucket. The woman nods and then sets off to the next pusher with me in tow holding the bucket. She repeats this over and over with the pushers as we gradually progress down Pusher Street towards Christiania's main entrance. There are probably about thirty pushers working this evening and all are willing to contribute cash for the building of the Children's House. As we make our way down the street the fact that the lady is drunk and making quite a ruckus alerts the pushers of our approach and many already have their cash donations out waiting to be dropped into the bucket before we even reach them. About half way down Pusher Street I realise that we will soon enter the domain of the rougher, meaner looking pushers towards the main entrance with their massive dogs, tattoos and menacing eyes. The lady doesn't seem at all concerned though and I am quite surprised that these pushers too are willing, even eager, to drop ever increasing amounts of cash into the Children's House bucket that I carry. Their dogs bark, but get swift kicks from their owners. A couple even hand me small pieces of hash as a reward for doing a good deed. Before long we have reached the end of Pusher Street and I am shocked to be holding a bucket absolutely stuffed full of money. I have to pack it down with my hand so as to ensure none of it flies out in the breeze. I try estimating how much is in the bucket, but it is impossible as some notes are scrunched while others are folded or rolled. Many of the notes are 100 kroner. I would guess that there would be well over three or four thousand Kroner in the bucket and all of it from this lady who has simply walked the length of Pusher Street telling all the pushers that the Children's House has run out of money. Even here amongst the anarchy of Christiania the pushers, while avoiding the reach of Danish law and authority, have to pay the TaxMum.

Arriving back at the party at the Children's House, we are cheered and patted on the back. The lady takes the bucket full of money and dumps all the notes onto a blanket where a couple of other mothers start counting the money out.

"My heeeeero!" jokes Gunner through a wide grin and hands me a beer as I sit down on the log next to him.

A PLACE IN LIFE

In the darkness of the early morning I had been listening to the rain fall on the roof of the Kosmic Bloomst. Now the rain has stopped and I watch the final beads of water cling to the glass of the windows. The clouds have turned the world into a grey-tinged gotham, although the birds still manage to sing beautiful harmonies. Under the floorboards rhythmic, soothing ambient music plays while a pot boils water on the tiny gas stove in the kitchen. Lonni passes me a steaming mug from halfway up the curved staircase then disappears down again without a word. The coffee, like so many other things in the village, is Moroccan. I lay in the dusty attic finding joy and relaxation. It seems that I have kicked my habit of distance and I feel no urge for movement. Christiania, for the time being, has stayed me when previously my hunger for distance and travel had kept me moving forward, never allowing me to stay in one place for long. I marvel at the fact that here I am in a three hundred year old attic with a steep dry roof and a mattress to sleep on. I've been here, in Christiania, long enough now to feel a slight touch of belonging. I no longer walk around awkwardly as the tourists do gawking at the unusual sights and shuffling uncomfortably by the pushers and their huge nasty dogs. Instead I have begun to sup with the drunks and toke with the pushers.

The door bangs downstairs, the signal that Nin and Franny have gone off to school for the day. Lonni's head emerges from the curved stairs leading down through the attic floor. She smiles one of her giant flashy smiles and asks how her tourist is.

"Great," I reply, "The W.C. Fields guys told me about a collective meeting today at the Bathhouse. They thought I might be able to pick up some work there."

"Those men," Lonni sighs feigning disgust. "Well, at least I'm glad that they are helping you. They can't be all that bad then."

I try to convey to Lonni that they aren't bad at all, they just like their beer and the company of other men. She won't have any of it, although I can see she has become a little more positive since they have been helping me.

"The baaaathhouse, huh?" Lonni explains emphasising the word with a throaty chuckle.

"What?"

"I neeeever go to the bathhouse unless I can help it, maybe once or twice in the winter maaaaybe. It's too….." as she searches for words my mind flashes to Nico, the gay guy whom I mistakenly went on a date with.

"Sleazy?" I add for her.

"Arrrrrrgh!" she laughs heartily almost spilling her coffee. "C'mon," she says with a big wave of her hand. "Leeeeeets smoke a joint, eh?"

And we smoke and talk and, as usual, before long she is remembering her singing lover. "You know we had it so right," Lonni says with a clear tenor of pain to her voice.

Lying on my back I stare out of the window framed in the rustic old wood of the attic, "Yeah?"

"On mornings like this, after the girls had gone to school we would smoke a joint in bed and make love all day. We had it so right, we knew each other so well that I would be coming the instant we started and would not stop for hours and hours."

Although I'm not looking directly at her I can sense the tear in her eye and almost feel it run down her check into the corner of her mouth. She wipes the tear away and stares out of the window across the tops of the trees and over the lake.

"Why don't you do a puzzle? Imagine your life falling back into place with each new piece you place down," I say, realising how lame the suggestion sounds the moment it comes from my mouth.

She replied, "I have too many other things to do."

"Like what?" I ask, knowing full well that she has nothing to do today.

She looks at me sadly, almost as if death is upon her, and says, "Like crying!"

I slide my hand over to where she rests hers on the broad wooden beams of the attic floor.

"Ohhhh, you are a nice tourist," she says with the hint of a smile. "But it is not just my luuuuver, it's also this place, Christiania. Life is just too hard and I have my girls who are growing up. Nin loves it, but Franny hates it. Each day I side with a different one of them. I just don't know what to do. When he took the money from Monsters, as you call it, people wouldn't talk to me anymore. Most wouldn't even look at me. It was as if I had taken it myself. People can be so cruel."

"I don't know, I've seen you 'Hi Hi-ing' all over the place," I protest.

"You don't understand, they'll be nice to my face, but behind my back they plot against me. But whoooooo knooows, it could just be part of the symphony and I am only the sad violin playing in the dark corner."

Lonni says many things like this, statements of sadness that shout her misery much louder than the soft voice by which she speaks of them.

PROTEST

Up at the W.C. Fields Clubhouse the old punks seem to be getting ready for something. Poo, Gunner and a few others are packing three pushbikes, the ones with boxes on a front axle, with crates of beer and their five-foot long chillum. One of the bikes is fitted with a full sized armchair onto which Poo climbs as though he is a king on his royal litter. Gunner climbs on the bike seat behind Poo and says to me, "You coming!" more like an order rather than a question.

I guess I am, "Where to?"

Both Gunner and Poo laugh and smile like children while keeping our destination a secret. The old punks ride their bikes, squeaking and swerving under the weight of men and beers, down Pusher Street to the main gates of Christiania. Without transport of my own I'm left to jog along beside them. We pass under the Christiania sign and find ourselves in the city. A canyon of five story high buildings unfolds before us as we continue our journey in a small convoy. City people stop to look at our motley crew and it is only when I am among city folk I realise how filthy and tatty my clothes are. Next to the old punks I am among peers, but out here in the city the contrast of cleanliness and clothing becomes very apparent. After a short journey that takes us along a canal and over a bridge we halt by the steps of a huge, grand old building. Business suits are walking up and down the wide sweeping entrance stairs as though they have many important matters to attend to.

"What are we doing here?" I ask anyone who will answer.

"Well," says Gunner, unhitching the crates of beer and giant chillum from the bike on which he was riding. "We are here to protest!"

As he tells me this I notice a couple of policemen walking towards us from higher up on the building's stairs. They appear annoyed at our arrival and speak curtly, in Danish, to the old punks. Poo waves them away as though they are annoying insects and continues to unload the beer and chillum from the bike. The police speak again, this time more forcefully, but they stop short of manhandling the old punks. They begin to argue and I am left on the fringe unable to partake in the foreign language discourse. The police are becoming very angry and are calling on their radio, the static adding to the official tone of their voices and the growing seriousness of the situation.

Not long after a police van pulls up on the street in front of the grand old building. Then a TV broadcast crew arrives; I assume they have been scanning the police radio frequencies. By this stage the old punks have filled their five-foot chillum full of hash and are putting a flame to it as Gunner kneels down using his lungs as bellows. A huge flame shoots from the top of the Chillum and a massive hash cloud rises as though the building has caught on fire.

Still I have no idea what all this public disobedience is in aid of.

"A protest," says Poo when he sees my troubled expression. "Anders, one of our friends, is in court today charged with importing hash into Denmark. A couple of months ago the boat he was crewing from the Middle East was searched when it arrived in Copenhagen. They had over a tonne of hash on board."

I whistle in amazement as another recently arrived blue van unloads its cargo of riot police in full armament of clubs, vests, shields and helmets. Then it's my turn on the chillum. Thankfully the police aren't quite yet organised and they only glare at me while I am puffing away at the giant wooden shaft. As I'm puffing I watch the police and I can see them getting ready for action. Out here in the city, away from Christiania, I feel vulnerable to the police and the fact that I am breaking the law by smoking a five-foot high chillum stuffed full of hash makes me nervous. The guys from the W.C. Fields Club don't seem phased by the police presence at all but they come from here, Denmark. Christiania is their home town and it is expected that they act this way. Lonni's description of me as a tourist has never felt as real as it does now. If I get arrested I don't have anyone to bail me out, or for that matter anyone within twenty thousand kilometres to make my one telephone call to, as Lonni doesn't even own a phone. If I'm arrested I am on my own and no doubt would be deported in a single bang of a judge's anvil. The hit from the chillum only serves to amplify such paranoia. So, as the riot police form a line and prepare to close down the protest, I slowly make my way to the rear of the old punks and then disappear into the crowd that has gathered to watch our blatant act of civil disobedience. The guilt of leaving the old punks to their fate holds me tight, but this isn't my fight. I don't even know the guy, Anders, who has been arrested and I am not quite ready to leave Denmark in the back of a Department of Immigration van just yet. Carmen always said to me, when I was about to do something crazy, that there is a fine line between courage and stupidity and it would only be stupid to get myself arrested out here in front of the courthouse.

ANARCHY RULES

All afternoon I have been chopping and mixing the ingredients for a pasta sauce that I hope to surprise Lonni with when she gets home from work. Outside, in the Kosmic Bloomst's courtyard, Nin and Franny have been playing with one of their school friends. Their friend appears so happy to be in Christiania and has wanted to speak to me, the tourist, all afternoon. Unfortunately, as the same with both Nin and Franny, she speaks no English and I no Danish. Even though her friend wanted to hang out around me, Franny seemed determined to take her outside away from my company. It is starting to concern me that I am unable to find any common ground with Franny. This is her home after all and I feel as though I am making her a little less comfortable in it.

There are several homes in the Kosmic Bloomst building and in Lonni's area her kitchen takes up approximately one third of the space. Only cold water runs from the tap so a big, blackened pot is used for constantly heating water. Underneath the bench and behind some tatty curtains is a pot that Lonni and the girls use to go to the toilet. That pot was the focus of most of the induction that Lonni gave to me when I came to live in her home.

"What eeeever you doooo," said Lonni to me when I first arrived. "Do not use that pot for coooooooking!"

"Why?" I asked. For an answer she shooed me to the far side of the kitchen bench then placed the pot on the floor and crouched over it so as I could see only her head poking above the kitchen bench. Then came a light tinkling of Lonni's pee splashing into the pot and she gave me a wide, cheeky grin as she emptied her bladder.

So I was careful finding a cooking pot and am just turning the gas bottle valve to bring the sauce down to a simmer when Lonni arrives home from work.

"Hi, hi," comes her voice as the old, thick wooden door swings open. "Ohhh, you are cooking me dinner."

"Least I can do," I remark while organising water to boil. It seems though it isn't as, Lonni continues to stare at me. A tear wells at the corner of her eye and runs down her cheek.

"Yooooou," Lonni cries out. "No one cooks for me, neeeeever." She accentuates the 'never' with a broad sweeping of her hand and then quickly closes the gap between us and squeezes me in a strong embrace.

"I wish Franny felt the same way about me," I say after Lonni had releases me. "She really doesn't like me being here."

"Ahhhhh, Franny," says Lonni and waves her hand as though to dismiss her daughter from her thoughts.

"Except that this is Franny's home, not mine. I don't think she wants me here."

"Franny is almost a teenager, I'm sure you can remember what that is like," Lonni says.

"Listen, Lonni, perhaps I shouldn't be here, you know I don't like making Franny feel uncomfortable."

"Forget Franny," Lonni uses that sweeping motion of her hand again.

"How can you say that, you're her mother…" I break off my words as I feel as though I am stepping over boundaries.

Lonni stands glaring at me as though I have insulted her. We stand in silence staring into each other's eyes. Slowly, Lonni's mouth turns up at the edges and she laughs, "What do you know, you're just a tourist."

And we both laugh. However, I feel that there is more to be talked about on the subject. For now I focus on cooking Lonni and the girls' dinner, happy that I can assist in the running of her home.

After dinner, Lonni leaves with the girls to take Franny's friend home to the city and I'm left to write in my notepad up in the attic listening to music, smoking cigarettes and drinking whisky. All of a sudden I hear the door downstairs swing open and a woman's voice shouts out, "Lonni!"

By the time I am down the stairs a woman is already well into the house. "Yeah, hi, Lonni's not home right now," I tell her.

"Who are you?" she speaks curtly to me. Then, without a pause for my reply, "Are you just another cunt, are you?"

As she says this I am squatting half way up the stairs peering down into her face. My eyes level off a foot above hers. We are not far apart and the small void between us had become extremely hostile. My first thought is to throw her out, but I have heard Lonni mention a crazy lady about the village who has the tendency to burst into people's homes uninvited so I restrain my instincts and instead stammer. "Um...er...I think you better leave."

I continue on down to the bottom of the stairs and by the way the woman is postulating I half expect her to physically attack me. She continues to yell abuse. "You fucking cunt, go find somewhere else to live you piece of shit!"

I do my best to usher her out through the door. I'm over six foot tall and she is less than five foot and very slightly built, so it isn't hard to use my size to back her out through the door. She is pretty worked up and still insulting me with shouts and pointed finger. I close the door in her face while she is still shouting. A moment later I think it best to put the bolt through the lock as she doesn't seem to be going away, just standing on the other side of the door hurling abuse. Through the door I hear Lonni's next door neighbour, Tommy. open his door which shares the same landing as Lonni's home. All hell breaks loose as Tommy starts shrieking at the top of his voice at the old lady. I sneak a look through the window to see that Tommy has driven the old woman to the ground with the sheer force of his verbal attack. He is turning red in the face shouting while standing over her as she attempts to crawl backwards in retreat. He stops shouting. Thick veins protrude from his neck. He stands threateningly above the woman with his hands on his hips. She gathers herself up and slinks away from the Kosmic Bloomst, all the while with her head turned towards him to ensure that he is not pursuing her. Once she's gone I open the door and thank Tommy.

"Oh," he says. "She's crazy and in her own way she is protecting Lonni. I shouldn't get so angry, but it just pisses me off that people have to stick their noses into other people's business all the time besides I know you are alright." And he gives me a pat on the shoulder before heading back into his section of the Kosmic Bloomst and closing the door behind him.

I notice another of Lonni's neighbors, old Bill, sitting by the fireplace in the middle of the Kosmic Bloomst's courtyard. He's sitting back with a big grin on his face having watched the drama unfold.

"Never boring in Christiania!" he says to me with the twang of an American accent, and I take it as an invitation for me to come and sit with him.

Lonni introduced me to Bill a while ago and told me that he was a bit of a solitary man and not to be surprised if he didn't acknowledge my presence, let alone talk to me. So I'm pleased that he has initiated conversation with me. He's old, but fit looking, a big man with a bear of a frame, although his movements are graceful and controlled making him less physically imposing than he might otherwise be. His presence is born of a sharp intellect that can be seen behind his eyes and through his thoughtful expressions. I sit next to him on a log and watch what he is doing. Laid out before him are rows of matchsticks which he continues to pick up and put down in various piles, meticulously counting the matchsticks in each pile before changing their arrangement by moving matchsticks from one pile to another.

"Whatchya doing?" I ask.

"I have a decision to make, the matches are helping," he tells me, but my quizzical expression conveys that his answer hasn't enlightened me at all as to his purpose. "Numerology," he continues, "using patterns in numbers to help divine an answer."

"What's the question?"

He changes the subject, "How are you finding it in Christiania."

"Great, besides that lady just now, I think it's amazing!"

"Don't worry about her. Every village has a crazy old woman poking her nose into other peoples business."

"You're American," I state. "How come you're here in Christiania?"

"Oh, man, I've been here for years, almost since it began in the seventies. I was a freelance journalist a long time ago and I came to Europe, for the first time, to report on the Czechoslovakia uprising in '68." he issues a small chuckle. "You see the Czechs thought that socialism needed a more humanistic and moderate flavor, but the Russians had other ideas and they sent in their tanks. So I came to report on it and I fell in love with Europe. You know it was the sixties and all the flower power shit was happening, both here and in America. However, here things were real, like raw man. Back home in the states it was all rich kids thinking they could change the world but not really having any idea what the world really was. Their inspiration was Flash Gordon and the Green fucking Lantern, fucking comic books! In Europe, man, they really knew about life, generations upon generations of the underclass, they rioted, took over buildings and were literally gunned down and run over by tanks for trying. America was like the candy floss of the sixties, Europe was the real deal, a real revolution, a real fight against the establishment. So, after the Czech uprising I stayed and drifted around Europe for a while, reporting and writing, freelancing for magazines, but mostly enjoying the people. Then one day I came to Denmark, discovered Christiania, met a girl and here I am. How about you?"

I tell him my story and he says, "Yeah, you can't just walk in here and stay, so many people try to 'cause everyone loves the place, unless they're straight of course, but you have to have an in somehow. Lots of people come and hang out and smoke pot hoping that someday they can find their way in, but not many do. You're one of the lucky ones. Christiania attracts all types and because there aren't any police, no authority, people are wary about who stays, who they let in. It used to be a lot different."

"How?" I ask.

"Well, for a while it was full of junk, drugs, heroin mostly, and it was horrible, shit everywhere, people dying, no sense of community, everyone scared, stealing and fighting, all the stuff that goes hand in hand with junk and fucking junkies. It's much better now, things have cleaned up and the junk, along with the junkies, are gone. You can see the children playing everywhere and I guess that is what makes it so much better; the kids out and about playing." Bill reaches down and moves a matchstick from one pile to the next.

"So, it's not really anarchy then." I say.

"What do you mean?"

"Well, if you can't have junk then that's a rule. Doesn't even having one rule mean that it is something else other than anarchy?"

"I see what you mean. Actually, Christiania has three rules: no drugs, no violence and no selling property. If you leave you just have to give your home away."

"Yeah, so three rules which mean people really aren't free, it isn't really anarchy."

Bill thinks for a moment, counts some matchsticks and moves a couple between piles. He looks up to me and says, "Well, anarchy, if you want a definition, is simply the belief that no one has the right to rule. Anarchy says that all systems try to justify their authority and anarchists believe that those systems are illegitimate. Now, consider the three rules of Christiania; first no drugs, and by the way, as I'm sure you have already noticed, here in Christiania hash is not considered a drug."

"Yes," I say. "I've already made that mistake and people have gotten quite aggressive in telling me that it isn't."

"Yeah," says Bill, moving another matchstick. "Just like no-one refers to alcohol or tobacco as a drug, here in Christiania hash is like that, but definitely not a drug in the same sense as heroin or speed. You think though, if a community is saturated with junk, like heroin as it used to be here in Christiania, two things happen: first, junkies are enslaved to the junk and are certainly not free, but that's a personal choice, or not, depending on how you see addiction, but more importantly the junk creates a very powerful system orientated around who controls the junk trade. It's not like hash, the pushers up on Pusher Street don't gun each other down for control of the hash trade, they exist peacefully side by side, not so with junk. When there was junk in Christiania, the biker gangs were fighting. It was a war for control of the junk trade. The Hells Angels pretty much won that war and for a while they more or less ran Christiania. So, you see, by rejecting the junk, Christiania was in fact rejecting the authority that ran the junk trade, they were rejecting the authority of Hells Angels. By the establishment of that rule: no junk, which seems contrary to anarchy, it actually promoted anarchy because it disallowed the authority of the Hells Angels. Make sense?"

"In a round about kind of way, but what about the selling of property, how does not being able to sell property promote anarchy?" I ask.

"Once again, by selling property, or by placing a monetary value on a property, a system needs to be created to sustain and protect that value. You know, in the straight world, more than half of the rules, the laws, are there to simply protect people's property. To protect the people that have from those who have not. If you have laws you need police and police can only operate within a system, so by rejecting the monetary value of property Christiania rejects the system, the laws, that protect that property. So, if you can't sell your home you don't really own it and therefore don't require laws to protect that ownership."

"And violence? The last rule?" I ask.

"Who wants to live with violence?" says Bill in his soft, peaceful voice as he moves another matchstick.

"Yeah, but it is still a rule," I say.

"I guess, but hey, nothing's perfect is it?" He laughs.

"Okay, then who enforces the rules? If Christiania has rules, how can they be rules if there is no authority to enforce them?"

"Good question, but the point is that there is no system that owns that authority."

"So how are they enforced then?"

"The community, you know, the people. The community in Christiania is not a system. Nothing could be more disorganised than Christiania!" Bill laughs and another match stick is moved. "Everyone has different opinions on how things should be done. There is a council that meets every so often, but they can decide whatever they like, I'll never listen to them. Christiania, really, is just a whole bunch of people doing what the fuck they like when they like. If someone disagrees with someone else about what they are doing then they simply argue."

"Or kick down a fence you're trying to build!" I say.

"Huh?" Bill questions.

"Well, I'm building a fence up at the Moonfisher and every day we build a little more then some guy comes along and kicks the fence down saying that there are too many fences in Christiania already."

Bill chuckles: "Exactly, I'm with him by the way, too many boundaries already, but you're right and it will go on until someone gives up. If the Moonfisher is more determined to build that fence than the guy is in kicking it down, then the fence will be completed. If the guy is more determined to kick it down than the Moonfisher is to build it, then it won't be. It's a very good example of how things are decided in Christiania. Argue, argue, argue, but at the end of the day, Christiania is a community and people want, or need, to belong to the community so they will argue to the limit of what will allow them to stay a part of the community." Bill moves a final matchstick into what appears to me to be a random pile and says, "Done."

"So what was your question?" I ask.

"Tomorrow I'm heading out to a farm in the country and I wanted to know if I should drop an acid trip or not, and evidently I shouldn't."

"But I thought drugs weren't allowed in Christiania?"

"Man, I wouldn't dream of taking acid here!" says Bill. "I'd get lynched."

WORK

A couple of days ago Poo stopped by while I was working on the Moonfisher fence to tell me that he had sorted some more work for me at the Bathhouse. So, here I am in my underwear in the Bathhouse working with Johan, a Nordic Viking kind of guy, quite short, but firmly built with long straight golden hair down past his shoulders. When I arrived he greeted me in his underwear so I stripped off, grabbed a long broom-like brush and began scrubbing the Bathhouse tiles. It is warm, hot actually, as a large furnace burns big logs in the small office area of the Bathhouse. Even though we are both in our underwear we quickly lather up a sweat. About an hour after we began a student turned up and shyly offered us a decent size block of hash: "I feel sorry for those doing the cleaning," he told us and then quickly left.

I don't mind the work as it makes me feel useful and puts cash in my pocket, but if that guy wants to give me a block of hash to help us on our way then so be it. After a few hours of steady work, Johan and I have scrubbed the dressing area, hosed down the showers and sinks with disinfectant, and wiped the mud off the wooden benches in the sauna. We spend the next few hours taking showers and laying in the beautifully hot sauna with a small metal bowl full of mud. I love to smear it all over my sweaty skin, up and down my arms, between my legs, the back of my neck and all over my face. It feels wonderful. I would never have imagined the absolute pleasures of heat, mud and sweat. When I get too hot I jump out of the sweltering sauna and stand, naked except for the mud, in front of an open window. I am no longer embarrassed about my nudity. In fact I am starting to feel quite liberated. As the cool breeze hits the mud it hardens to create a crusty outer shell on my skin. Once I'm all crusted up I jump in the shower and wash all the mud off. Then repeat, two or three times more. Heaven.

TOURISTS

I often find myself walking past the red railway container that's home to the old man with crazy hair and piles of junk. When I first saw him, on my first day, he hardly noticed me. I was just another tourist walking around Christiania spellbound by its beauty and there are always an abundance of tourists in Christiania. In fact I am told that Christiania is the second most popular tourist attraction in Denmark after Tivoli, the world's oldest fun park. Christiania is, more or less, a fun park, no rides, but there certainly are a lot of attractions and side shows. Not to mention the abundance of clowns, I would hazard a guess that there would be more clowns here than in Tivoli. I'm not insulting the Christianites, there are literally lots of people dressed up as clowns in Christiania. They're never really doing anything clownish, just going about their business shopping at Grøntsagen, buying hash or mingling with the tourists.

It is only after this old man in his red railway container has seen me many times, has recognised that I'm not just a tourist, that he takes careful notice of me when I pass by. At first he hardly afforded me a glance, but the more I see him the more he appears to watch me. I can almost see his mind working behind his eyes attempting to figure me out, attempting to understand if I am harmless or a threat. The people I have met, like Lonni, the Moonfisher and Monster collectives, and the old W.C. Fields punks, are all very friendly. They know me, but this old guy, he doesn't and he can't afford to trust me. With no police to offer protection from a stranger who isn't leaving the old man sees me as potential danger, a threat to be wary of and keep his eye on.

KALLE

"Tourist," yells Lonni before she has even walked through the door. I can hear her arriving through the Kosmic Bloomst courtyard, her feet scrunching the gravel. "I will get work for yoooou!"

The rustic old door swings open and there's Lonni flashing a grin behind a brown paper shopping bag.

"Where," I ask with a little excitement.

"Follow me," and with a little mischievous smile she puts her groceries on the kitchen table.

"Doing what?" I have little patience.

Lonni remains silent, but her mischievousness grows. Having obtained my attention she simply turns and walks back out the door into the courtyard and continues down the dirt road through Dussen, past the outhouse and the footbridge and into South Dussen, the farthermost reaches of Christiania. We walk for about a kilometre along the dirt road winding between old buildings. Some are similar to the Kosmic Bloomst, a relic from the military past, others built with haphazard architectural imagination. We pass the red railway container and the old man comes out to see who is passing. "Hi, hi, Sventen," says Lonni.

The old man smiles with a beaming energy in his eyes and says a quiet, joyful greeting back to Lonni. When he sees me following up behind his relaxed posture straightens, but quickly softens again as Lonni smiles at me and he realises I am her friend. Lonni motions her hand at the old man as if to wave away his suspicions and continues walking.

"What? Where?" I keep asking periodically as I follow the tall, slim and giggling Dane down the dirt road, overwhelmed with curiosity.

Lonni waits for me, crossing her arms as she turns. "I'm not sure that I have work for you," she confesses. "But today I am feeling strong. You have been sooooo gooood for me and I understand how Christiania works, I can do this!"

She turns and sets off again. I'm intrigued.

The trees lining the dirt road arch over the path providing a cool shade. Birds chirp unseen in the foliage and leaves rustle in the breeze. Lonni turns and says, "Okay wish me luck."

"Good luck, of course but what are you doing?"

Lonni has stopped in front of a house. It is tall and narrow. The upper level of the house is a little wider than the bottom and it leans to the left a little. The geometric differences are only slight and I don't know if I am seeing them correctly, it is as though my brain is confused by the house. I basically see a rectangular cube and my brain wants to believe it but the geometric proportions do not quite make sense. I wait on the dirt road while Lonni climbs the front stairs to the odd little house's front porch and raps her knuckles against the door. Nothing happens and Lonni knocks again. We hear some cluttered stumbling from behind the door and a heavy lock being undone. The door swings inwards and despite the dim light I make out a stocky, solidly built guy in his late twenties. "Hi Lonni," he says in a polite but questioning tone. He does not appear to notice me standing on the dirt in the shade.

"We need something Kalle!" says Lonni.

Kalle looks puzzled and then quickly spots me in the shade. "What do you need?" Kalle speaks quickly with a deep voice, intense eyes and a thick Danish accent.

"This tourist needs some work," Lonni says quite forcibly.

"Yeah...well." Kalle hesitates, having been put on the spot by Lonni.

"Looooook," says Lonni. "I know business is good up on Pusher Street. I know some pushers and they have looooots of cash. If business is good for them it must be good for you too."

Kalle's pride inflates a little.

Lonni pauses a moment then continues, "You do good business because of Christiania. You need to put back in by giving this tourist some work."

"Okay," says Kalle. "I hear you. I guess I need some grass over there." He points to a flat area off to the left hand side of the porch.

"Also, the tourist is staying with me at the Kosmic Bloomst and I have two young girls. One has just started her period. He is fine, a good guy, but my girls need their privacy now. I know your wife and daughter have gone, do you have any room for the tourist?" Lonni asks.

I can't believe how bold she is being. After a moment pause, he frowns and says, "Yes, he can stay downstairs. There is a bed down there.

It is messy and with lots of junk, but he can stay there." Kalle looks across to me. "Bring your things tomorrow morning and you can start." With a nod to Lonni and another glance at me, Kalle closes the door. Lonni turns to me smiling one of the biggest grins I have ever seen.

"Genius," is all I can say.

TAKING FROM THE GOVERNMMENT

For weeks I have been trying to find work in Christiania. I've had some luck at Monsters restaurant with a couple of lunches and dinners exchanged for dishwashing and the spring clean. There is occasional work cleaning the Bathhouse, building the fence around the Moonfisher park and now gardening for Kalle. It all seems to be happening now. Following my initial surf into Christiania a few months ago my wave broke and I have been paddling around searching out a new wave. Now it has found me. The momentum of my wave is carrying me forward.

Lonni and I lay in the attic smoking cigarettes and drinking coffee. Above us stars shine through large windows in the A-frame roof.

"I think I can fall in love with a wave," says Lonni.

"A wave?" I ask, thinking that I'll miss her when I move to Kalle's place.

"Yeah, the ocean or maybe a waterfall, you know the surging of water. Power and beauty, I could fall in love with it."

"Are you cold?" I ask.

"Yeeeees," says Lonni through gritted teeth, faking a shiver, "I have a heater."

"Where? I'll get it."

"Weeeeeeeell," she says, "I shouldn't really use it."

"Why not?"

"It's electric," She says with a look of shame.

"And..."

"I shouldn't have said anything about the heater, I forgot you are a tourist."

I laugh at being called a tourist, "What's wrong with an electric heater?"

"Well," says Lonni with a scornful look. "In Christiania some people think that we shouldn't use electricity because it comes from the government."

"Really."

"Some people say if Christiania takes things from the government then it allows the government to say that they are supporting us and argue that their laws should apply and the police should be allowed to come in. So I take the water and I take the electricity for the lights, I cook from a gas bottle. I used to take the electricity for the heater when my lover was here." As the thought of her lover enters her mind Lonni's whole body shrinks back into itself. Her confidence dissipitates and tears glaze over her eyes. She pauses for a moment, oblivious to my presence and stares out the window. After a long pause she returns her attention to me and continues. "If people in Christiania found out I was using an electric heater they would shout at me and tell everyone. That, on top of what my lover did, might have people wanting to kick me out"

"But you said that you use the electricity for the lights, and the TV, what's so different about the heater?" I say.

"The lights don't use much electricity, neither does the TV, but the heater uses a lot. Christiania pays money to the government for water and some of the electricity we use, but not all of it. The more electricity we use the more the government says that they are supporting us. If I were to use the electricity and people in Christiania found out they would accuse me of living off of the government and making is harder for Christiania to survive."

"It's not that cold," I say.

And it isn't.

GRASS

Having packed my bag in the attic of the Kosmic Bloomst I kiss Lonni on the cheek, give her a hug and walk along the dirt road down to Kalle's geometrically strange little house. The sun shines, the birds chirp and it's a great day. I have friends, I have work, more and more as each day passes, and I have found a place in the world that fits me comfortably. The straight world, as Lonni calls it, is absent from Christiania's village life. The city seems only to exist in another dimension and I hardly ever think about it.

As I approach the railway container the old man, Sventen, rises from a chair under a tree to observe my passage past. Now that he knows me to be Lonni's friend his suspicion and wariness has been replaced by a keen observation as though he is studying me with a scientific eye. He doesn't say 'hi hi' when I do, but his eyes are friendly.

Reaching Kalle's I wonder if I ever will get used to the slightly wider second story and the hardly perceivable lean to the left. I knock on his door.

"Hi, hi," Kalle yawns as he opens the door wearing only a pair of jeans. Squinting, with dark bags under his eyes, he is obviously hung-over. His muscular arms, chest and shoulders must be the result of great effort with weights and he seems a lot younger than I thought when I first saw him yesterday.

"Follow me," he says stepping out onto the front porch and continuing around the side of his house where a steep uneven slope takes us to his backyard. About three metres from the back of his house is a narrow canal that runs the entire length of Dussen. Built three or four hundred years ago, the canal was a defensive measure for the military against the Swedes. Kalle pulls a set of keys from his pocket and unlocks a padlock securing a door. It opens to reveal a small room filled with all sorts of junk: scuba tanks, a motorbike tire, a push bike, an old World War II German soldier's helmet. Tucked into one corner is an old mattress resting on a steel wire mesh bed frame. "Here you go. It is messy, but you can sleep there."

While it is not exactly the Hilton, it is more than I have had to sleep on in the past and it is secure. "Perfect," I say to Kalle. "Really appreciate it."

I dump my bag inside and then turn to Kalle to ask, "So, what work can I do?"

"This way," he says, proving to be a man of few words. He walks along the canal and up a slope to an area on the left hand side of his house. "I want grass here," Kalle says indicating a wide flat area at the end of his front porch. An old Labrador dog slowly tries to get up to greet Kalle.

"Hi Tina," says Kalle to his dog.

The poor old thing has tufts of hair falling out and both her eyes are clouded over with a milky-white haze. Tina barely manages to stand up and staggers, attempting to maintain balance.

"Grass," I say to myself.

"Grass," repeats Kalle.

"Smokeable grass?" I question.

And Kalle laughs. "No, normal grass."

"Well," I continue doing my best to sound as though I know all about growing grass. "There is too much shade in this area. I think we will need to thin out some of the tree branches hanging overhead and I will need to get some seeds. Do you have a chainsaw?"

"No," says Kalle. "But the Machine Hall in Christiania should be able to rent you a chainsaw and the Green Hall will have grass seeds and anything else that you need."

The Green Hall sells things for building and gardening and is located next to Grøntsagen, where I first met Lonni. I am unsure of the exact function of the Machine Hall, but I know it to be the first big building on Pusher Street, the big barn near the main gates to the city.

Kalle thrusts his hand into a pocket in his jeans and pulls out a thick wad of Danish kroner bound in a tight roll with an elastic band. He counts off a number of hundred kroner notes and gives them to me. "Take this for the chainsaw and the grass seeds, the rest of it for your first wages. Okay?"

"Okay," I respond, happy to have a decent amount of cash in my hand for the first time in a long while.

With a final grunt from beneath his hangover, Kalle heads back across his front porch towards the door. Before he disappears inside he turns and says, "Oh, and don't mess with the dog. She's very old."

I look at Tina who has settled back down into the dirt and appears to be asleep. Around her is a large hollow in the dirt that indicates this is her spot, right in the middle of where Kalle wants his grass. I see the challenge right away, how to grow grass where Tina the dog has priority for resting her weary old bones? I'll worry about that later, as right now I'm just glad to have a secure, private place to sleep and more work.

THE MACHINE HALL

I am on a mission for a chainsaw. A mission that invigorates me as power tools have a special place of worship within a young man's psych and a chainsaw is the veritable king of all power tools. I make my way over the wooden bridge from Dussen and into the heart of Christiania, past the Bathhouse and the Moonfisher Café and onto Pusher Street. As usual the drunks sup their wine and the dogs laze about as though they own the place.

I say "Hi, hi," to a few of the pushers I have come to know, but as I move further down Pusher Street among the meaner looking Pushers I don't issue greetings, just hold their gaze for a fleeting moment before quickly directing my sight elsewhere.

Between the last pusher and Christiania's main gate, Pusher Street widens and gradually loses its form. On the left runs a path past a three story building that contains Loppen, one of Christiania's bars that often plays live bands, and a number of small businesses, including Christiania Bikes and a vintage car restoration workshop. To the right of Christiania's front gate is the large wooden barn that is the Machine Hall. The wooden boards that form its walls are faded and splintering and appear to be only just holding onto the nails that secure them. About to walk into the Machine Hall I see Aneka, the blond girl from Detlifs party whose friend got me so drunk I fell off a log, pushing her bike under the Christiania gate at the entrance to the city. I've seen her around a few times, but never found the chance to speak to her although I've always wanted to. "Aneka," I shout, a little too eagerly, and wave as she notices me.

"Oh, hi," she says.

"Do you want to grab a cup of tea at the Moonfisher?" I ask, cringing at how hopeful I sound.

"Can't, I've got work to do," she says gazing past me down Pusher Street.

"Oh yeah, where do you work?"

"I clean Detlif's house for him. Look, I've got to go," she says, turning her back and mounting the bike. She rides away bouncing over the cobblestones.

I watch her go, she doesn't look back.

One of the Machine Hall's massive barn doors is ajar and I walk through into a vast space shaded from the sunlight. Farm and mechanical equipment are strewn around, engine hoists, tractor drills and spare tires. The space is one giant room except for a narrow and not too sturdy looking staircase that begins almost in the middle of the space and reaches up to the right wall, tracing it all the way up to a small loft office suspended high off of the ground. A not unpleasant musky smell lingers in the air, adding a hint of rustic nostalgia to the machinery. Dust particles float in a wonderfully rich slice of sunlight that penetrates the space through a row of skylights up in the roof. "Helloooo," I say loudly. I can't see any signs of life.

Nothing.

"Hellooooo," louder still.

A creak issues from up high where the rickety staircase meets the office and a door opens. A great waft of smoke comes through the open door and hangs in the light coming through the skylights. "Who's that?" issues forth a French accent before a big burly man steps out of the office and onto the stair's landing.

"Me," I say, standing just within the Machine Hall's huge doors.

"Oui, but who?" asks the man again as he brushes long, curly hair off of his face.

"I'm looking to hire a chainsaw and was told that I should come here to the Machine Hall."

"For massacring people?" he asks, not appearing to be joking.

"Only trees," I say, smiling at both our wits.

"Cutting trees in Christiania is almost as bad as the cutting up people," he shouts down. "Actually, come to think of it, I'd rather you cut some of the people with it. Come up."

I walk to the base of the narrow stairs and the closer I get the less I feel inclined to trust them with my weight. I look up at the man standing way above me and judge him to be at least twice as heavy as me, if they can carry him then they must be able to carry me. I begin my accent and can see that each of the wooden planks laid across to form the stairs has hollows that have been gradually worn by people's feet over the years.

One step, then two, and the staircase holds, although I can feel a slight sway as I progress further up its height around the wall. By the time I reach the top the man has disappeared back into the office. I follow him in and see him place a long, slender joint onto an ashtray. He swivels his chair to face the entrance, where I remain, and blows another cloud of smoke out through his nostrils before saying, "Come in, sit down."

The office has a large round table with old wooden chairs. I sit down and the joint is passed across. I smoke, splutter and say, "Yeah, well, I've been asked to help grow some grass down in Dussen and I need to chop some branches off trees so the sun can get through."

"Grass, grass; or grass, grass?" asks the man looking at me under a stern brow.

"Just grass," I tell him.

"Oh," he says, "Who for, you're not from Christiania?"

"No, I'm a tourist. For Kalle."

"For Kalle, eh?" Understanding that I am working for Kalle appears to issue a slight change in the man. He opens his posture to me a little more and seems to take a keener interest. He reaches out his hand and says, "Eric, my name is Eric. What sort of work do you do?"

"Anything really," I say.

"And you want a chainsaw," he states. "We have one and I can rent it to you for fifty kroner a day." He takes another long toke on his joint and passes it across to me while tilting his head back and ejecting the smoke up into the ceiling.

"Great, can I take it from now through to tomorrow afternoon?" The joint passes back to Eric and he nods while toking again.

Eric gets up and walks to the landing above the stairs, motioning for me to follow him. I hesitate to follow too closely as I am unsure if the structure will hold both of us at the same time. The stairs creak and groan loudly as Eric descends and I can see them sway as he reaches the point where they cease to trace the wall and begin their unsupported traverse to the centre of the Machine Hall. Eric peaks over his shoulder with a smirk as though he senses my fear, yet at the same time having confidence in the aging structure. I follow him genuinely fearing that the whole staircase will collapse beneath us.

Eric produces a chainsaw and a tin of petrol from a cluttered shelf and I dig a fifty kroner note out of my pocket. "Do you know who Kalle is?" he asks.

"Not really, I've only just met him," I reply, a little suspicious of the question.

Eric smiles and I can tell he has no intention of explaining Kalle any further to me. He changes the subject. "If you need more work, the Machine Hall needs someone on Thursdays to help with the garbage run. You interested?"

"Sure am," I respond excitedly, "What day is it today?"

"Ha, today is Tuesday, be here in two days. You are a foreigner, yes, not from Denmark, no?"

"No, not from Denmark. Why?"

Eric tilts his head and swipes his long black curls away from his face. "So you don't take the pension from the government?"

"No, I don't take any government money," I say, wondering why he is asking.

"Good," says Eric, with a big smile. "Me neither, so we pay you more. Less if you take government money, more if you don't. We will pay you three hundred kroner for four hours work. Okay?"

"Okay," I say smiling back at him, proud that I am not living off government money.

We shake.

I spend the rest of the day five metres off the ground, stripped to my shorts, leaning awkwardly out into space chopping off tree branches with the king of all power tools.

THE KNOWLEDGE

Lonni bangs at the door waking me, for the first time, in the dusty little junk room under Kalle's house. She squashes her face against the small window high in the wall, waves her hands and shouts at me to get up. It takes a little while for me to fully come together as I sit dazed on a empty beer crate and splash water on my face while Lonni chatters away. I am unable to piece together what she is trying to tell me, but eventually I am awake enough to follow her up the side of Kalle's house and begin to fathom that she wants to take me somewhere.

"Come on," she says, grabbing my arm to haul me up the slope.
"Where?" I ask again.
"To meet Sventen, I already told you."
"The old guy in the railway wagon?"
"Yes, Sventen. He can tell you about The Knowledge."

Still rubbing snot from my eyes I can barely comprehend what Lonni is saying let alone some all-encompassing mystical information that I assume The Knowledge to be. I follow Lonni down the path that loosely winds its way around thick tree trunks close to the lake's edge and pass a row of houses similar to a terrace, but roughly built like those of a shantytown. Not to say that the houses are dilapidated. On the contrary, most of them are well cared for and painstakingly built, using odd angles and wild ratios, chaos rather than conformity. One is painted like a sixties acid trip with Jim Morrison strolling through the desert about to be consumed by a huge fire breathing dragon. Another is moulded like an igloo and would suite Greenland more than the tall water reeds by this pretty little lake.

The path runs through the courtyard of an old building that resembles a barn, only its walls are made of thick stone. Its structure is L shaped and has a steep A-frame roof with little windows poking out. Just after the barn is Sventen's home. The railway container is dug about a foot into the earth, small pot plants are arranged on wire mesh shelves near the front door, which is open. Inside it is dark and difficult to see past a shelf full of tools and implements. A quite shuffling comes from deeper within as Lonni bangs on the side of the metal container and says, "Hi, hi. It's me, Lonni."

From out of the darkness emerges Sventen, wearing an old red T-shirt with several holes in it and striped pyjama bottoms. He is tall and slim, looking fit for an old man. His forehead continues all the way over his scalp in between wild locks of silver hair that shoot out from above each ear. He speaks Danish to Lonni in a jovial tone and turns to me, smiles and says, "Hello."

"Hi, hi," I say back, unsure of myself.

"Sventen," Lonni says to me. "He used to follow my guru too." She turns to Sventen. "I have come to ask if you will tell our tourist here The Knowledge." Lonni is looking at him with great respect and expectation.

Sventen pauses for a moment as his expression becomes thoughtful. He appraises me, passing his observant gaze all over my body, above it and behind it then looks deep into my eyes for a period of time in which I become unsettled. He steps back, takes an elbow in one of his hands and scratches his head with the other. "He is not ready to receive The Knowledge. Sorry, no." he says and returns to his jovial state, all seriousness gone.

Lonni looks at me with a sad face and says, "Sorry."

An awkward silence develops between us, only Sventen is smiling. There is not much more for anyone to say on the subject so I say goodbye to both Lonni and the smiling Sventen and make my way, shoulders slumped and feet scuffing in the dirt, to the Bathhouse and the sauna's warm embrace, where I wonder what Carmen is doing at this moment. Is she in some old Scottish pub with a pint of Guinness giggling to the lame jokes of a guy with a roguish accent or sunning herself on an exotic South American beach eyeing off a bronzed Adonis in a thong stuck up between his arse cheeks? Either way, she is not with me. I wish she was.

OUTLAW

Walking back to my room under Kalle's place from the Bathhouse, I hear police sirens down at the end of Dussen. I've just stepped off of the footbridge that crosses the lake and onto the dirt path that runs to the Kosmic Bloomst to the right and Kalle's place to the left, an area thick with trees that is abuzz with the chirping of birds. It is usually such a peaceful place, but today the sirens drown out the birds and are an unpleasant reminder that the city is not far away. The dirt path runs a couple of kilometres through Dussen and eventually intersects a city street in an industrial area of Copenhagen. The whirring and squealing of the siren is getting louder and, although it is hard to judge, it sounds as though the police are close to the edge of Christiania. A second then a third siren kick up from different proximities within the city, converging towards Christiania at the end of the dirt path. It sounds as though the whole city has gone mad with a police chase. Despite the cacophony, it is only pollution to my ears as it is happening in that other dimension, that other reality that exists parallel to Christiania, out there in the city.

I continue along the path scuffing my heels in the dirt as I follow its twists and turns around the three big-barn like buildings, identical to the Kosmic Bloomst, that sit on the lake's edge at this end of Dussen. The police sirens grow louder, corrupting an otherwise beautiful day. Passing the last barn the dirt path straightens out and I can see all the way down to the end of Dussen. There, pushing his Harley Davidson, is Kalle. The sirens have stopped wailing, but I can see the bright strobing of blue lights reflected off of the treetops.

"Fucking police!" Kalle yells out from a distance as we approach each other.

"What? Were they after you?" I shout back with more than a little smile growing across my face.

"Sure were, but they weren't fast enough today though, those pussies," he smiles back and stops pushing his Harley as I come to stand beside him.

His Harley has slightly extended forks and is covered with chrome that shines and glints in the sunshine. Fuck the Law is painted in big black letters on the white fuel tank and underneath the writing a hand is painted with the middle finger extended. Fuck the Law is also written on the back of his helmet in big bold letters.

"Where are they?" I ask, wondering why the police aren't still chasing him as he pushes his bike along the dirt path.

"Who?" Kalle asks, not quite understanding the question.

"The police."

"Ha, those fuckers wouldn't dare come into Christiania. They're probably still down at the end of Dussen scratching their balls, not knowing what to do next."

"What's wrong with your bike?"

"Huh?"

"How come you're pushing it?"

"You know the rules in Christiania, no cars, or motorbikes. It really shits me actually as it is a long way to push this thing." Kalle stands up a little straighter stretching out his shoulders and relaxes with only one hand holding the bike up. The heavy bike starts to slip away from his grip. "Crap," shouts Kalle, scrambling to catch it before it falls, but failing. It crashes heavily to the ground sending a fine mist of dust billowing out in all directions.

"Give me a hand will you?" asks Kalle as he bends over to pick up the bike.

Together we struggle to get the bike upright again. Kalle catches me laughing as we hoist it up. "What are you laughing at?"

"Well, here you are with Fuck the Law written on your bike and helmet, leading the police on a chase and escaping into Christiania, but here you obey the rules by not riding your bike."

"Yeah, well," Kalle doesn't seem to quite know how to respond. "I need Christiania. I don't need the law. If I were to ride my bike in here I would have every man and his dog at my front door yelling at me, and believe me, you don't want to have that happen to you in Christiania."

"Do you have any hash on you?" I ask.

"No, but there's some at my place. I'm not going there though just in case the police are calling in the riot squad to come and get me, I'm going to Nemoland for a while. Here's my key, you'll find it on the top shelf in the big room."

"Thanks, take care, I'll come to Nemoland if I see any police."

Without any farewells Kalle is already pushing his bike down the dirt path towards the footbridge that leads over the lake to Nemoland. I let myself in, going upstairs to look for the hash. Reaching up to the top shelf of his cupboard my hand grabs hold of the butt of a shiny silver handgun. I press a button on its side and a magazine ejects from out of its handle, fully loaded. Next to the gun are four great blocks of hash, each the size of a house brick. I choose a chillum from Kalle's wide selection and spend the rest of the day smoking and getting the soil ready at the side of his house.

FOR QUEEN AND COUNTRY

Lonni and I lean back against the rough surface of a log, shoulders touching. We each have a beer in hand and our feet scuff small trenches in the dirt. Children play all around in the grounds of Christiania's school for small children where Lonni sometimes lends a helping hand. There is a party for the children tonight and they scamper all over an old wooden boat that has been placed in the school's playground. It has a thick pole that imitates a mast with a crow's nest at its top that the children delight in climbing up into. Lonni's kids, Nin and Franny, are a little older than most of the children but they laugh and play with the little ones among the lush foliage of the trees surrounding this beautiful little glade. The adults sit by a fire and talk animatedly while sipping at beers and handing out sausages on slices of bread whenever a hungry little kid, covered in dirt, appears.

I have no idea which children belong to which adults, as one moment a little girl will be cuddling with one man and the next climbing on the shoulders of another. A scruffy little boy will hug a woman tight, who I assume to be his mother, then moments later he is scolded by another, while still another woman pulls out a hanky to wipe snot from his nose. While each of the children must have their parents nearby, they truly appear to belong to each and every adult, or rather, to Christiania itself. They are the children of the Free Town, allowed to run free with a parental confidence for safety that I have never seen out in the straight world. The children's parents appear to be confident that Christiania will look out for them, protect them and provide the love and comfort that all little children need. It may be the alcohol warming my blood, as I have certainly drunk enough of it tonight, but I see a huge amount of love and pride among the adults as they watch Christiania's newest generation run amok amongst the playground.

The sun has been setting for most of the evening and finally the sky has turned a darker shade of blue. Many of the little kids have fallen asleep on adult laps, and one has even curled up in a little ball snuggled in between Lonni and me to draw warmth from our bodies. His mother, I can only assume, leans over and picks him up from under his armpits. He does not open his eyes as he is carried like a slumping rag doll and gently lowered into the front box of a Christiania bike. Lonni waves to the lady as Nin and Franny appear by her side and issue forth an excited stream of Danish. Lonni answers them while nodding and hugs them both before turning to me to say, "They are staying at a friend's house tonight, I am free!"

"Good," I say. "I need someone to cheer me up."

"Are you still upset about Sventen not giving you The Knowledge?" she asks.

I sigh. "I guess I am. It's not like I really wanted to know it, but the fact that he wouldn't tell me…"

"Don't be upset. I think Sventen is jealous that you're my friend. He always wanted me to be his girlfriend in the old days, even now."

"Bloody Knowledge," I say.

Lonni's grin stretches to that immense size that only her face could accommodate. "C'mon, I'll by you another beer." She stands up shaking her legs to loosen the muscles after sitting for so long.

I try to stand, but fail totally. We have been sitting for so long and drank so many beers that my legs refuse to support me and I have to take a step back to keep balance. The log we had been leaning against trips me and I fall flat on my back laughing. Lonni is laughing too, she leans over the log and holds out her hand. I take it and pull, but rather me going up she comes down and falls over the log on top of me. We laugh and laugh covered in dirt and twigs and I realize just how drunk we have become at this children's party.

Gradually, with much stumbling and tripping, grasping at each other to stay upright, we make our way towards the centre of the village to have beers and shots at Nemoland among the unbranded bikers. Music pumps and the punters are jiving and bopping in drunken revelry. Lonni throws her hair around in wild swirls and grabs at my arm in an attempt to get me to dance with her. I try to keep time with the music but my mood won't allow me to sync with the beats as I can't shake the feeling of rejection that Sventen has wrought over me. As the bar grows busier the punters squeeze together. I bounce between massive tattooed arms and shoulders like a pinball until I reach the bar and order another beer and shot of tequila. Shot down and midway through the beer Lonni dances over, takes one look at my sullen face grabs my elbow and drags me outside to sit on a bench by a fire in a steel drum.

"You doing okay?" she asks. "You're looking a little green."

I can't answer, fearing that if I open my mouth it won't be words coming out. The best I can do is issue a low groan.

"C'mon," says Lonni, lightly punching my arm. "You're tougher than that." She's in great form, still shuffling her feet in time to the music with that gigantic grin pasted across her face.

I burp, dangerously close to puking, and feel the need to lay down. I crawl up onto the wooden table top and roll onto my back. "Just puke," Lonni says.

Taking her advice I roll onto my stomach with my head hanging off of the end of the table and open my mouth to let a warm stream of tequila-flavored beer splash down into the dirt. "Go boy, that's the spirit, yeeeeha!" whoops Lonni giving me a couple of hard slaps on the back as still more beer flows out from my innards. "We can't stop yet, I don't get the chance go out much. Let's go, I'll buy you another beer at Woodstocks."

I groan again as I know that Woodstocks is most definitely not for the fainthearted. However, with the last beer and tequila I drank now soaking into the dirt I am feeling a little better and Lonni is right, with her kids to look after she hardly ever gets the chance to go out. I owe it to her to keep the night going. Rolling off of the table I wipe the remnants of puke from my lips and do my best to scrape it from my hair. I stand up straight bend over to touch my toes and bounce into a couple of star jumps. Lonni laughs. I swallow another burp and tell her, "Okay, good to go, where's my beer?"

Lonni places her hands in the small of my back and pushes me across to Woodstocks on the other side of Pusher Street. I have been in Christiania for close to five months now and I have not been back into Woodstocks since the first night I arrived. While Nemoland and the Moonfisher welcome and provide for the tourists in Christiania, Woodstocks has an insular crowd that does not welcome strangers. I have come to see it as the home of professional drinking frequented by those who start drinking in the morning and continue all day long until a wild party of the truly and absolutely drunk rages into the early hours of the next day. The Woodstock crowd are the hardest of the hardcore drinkers. I would never consider going into Woodstocks alone, but tonight I am happy to follow Lonni's lead and besides, I feel that I have earned my entry tonight by already having puked in the dirt and very nearly passed out on a table. While I don't consider myself to be a hardcore drinker, right now I am as hardcore as I am ever going to get. So what the hell, Woodstocks here we come.

Lonni swings the double-hinged doors open to reveal a party in full swing, a party that has most probably been raging continuously for the past twenty-five years. The room isn't nearly as crowded as Nemoland, but what it lacks in density it certainly makes up in intensity. In the middle of the room an old couple is locked arm in arm at the elbow, swinging around and around. Centrifugal forces make it difficult for them to place their feet in the next required spot in order to maintain balance, but somehow they manage to stay upright. They move around the floor in a random pattern as though they are dancing an underclass version of a ballroom waltz. Most of the other drinkers are able to stay out of their way, but they collect one man in their mad spinning who momentarily gets caught up in their dance, before being flung off into the far wall with his beer sloshing over the floor. He doesn't appear at all perturbed as if it is just one of the acceptable dangers of drinking in Woodstocks. Despite the couple pirouetting around the room the music is barely audible over the cacophony of drunkard arguments emanating from small groups scattered around and tucked into dark corners. As with the music, the furniture has been kept to a minimum, probably for the best as no one seems to walk a straight line. For every two steps forward people take they invariably take at least one step sideways. Music and furniture, I guess, are only things to get in the way of the serious business of drinking. While I felt drunk at Nemoland among the bikers, here in Woodstocks I feel positively sober in comparison to the room's occupants.

Lonni takes hold of my shirt collar and drags me across to the bar. "Two Tuborgs Sven," she shouts above the drunks to the barman.

"Hiya Lonni, how you been," Sven yells back while uncapping a couple of dark green bottles.

I turn to lean on the bar, watching the drunken spectacle while Lonni talks to Sven. The twirling couple finally spins into something solid enough to stop their motion, a pole in the middle of the room. The woman hits it with her head and stops dead with a bemused look on her face as though she's wondering what hit her. She appears not to see the pole at all and searches around the room looking for a culprit, while holding her hand to a large red welt on her forehead. He partner is still spinning with his elbow hitched high seemingly oblivious to having lost his partner, but without the woman countering his balance he is flung off towards a wall as his legs collapse underneath him.

At the other end of the bar two men are arguing loudly in Danish, neither listening to what the other says, just shouting and pointing while slowly turning red in the face. I turn back to face the bar and notice, high up on the wall above a row of almost empty liquor bottles, a framed picture of an old lady with a crown on her head. A drunk nearby notices where my gaze is directed and holds his beer up to me in a toast. "To Queen Margrethe the second!" he says loudly.

"To the Queen," I repeat and swig down a mouthful of beer.

"We love our Queen, we do," continues the drunk slightly drooling out of one side of his mouth. "She is a fine woman, a good Queen. All over the world where you find Danish people you will find a photo of the Queen. We may leave our country, but we Danes won't ever leave our Queen."

"Like here in Christiania," I say.

"Hey?" the drunk staggers a little.

"Well, like here in Christiania, it is sort of a different country to Demark. You don't recognize their laws and the back of the sign over Christiania's main gates says: You are now entering the EU. It's as though Christiania is a different country, but here is the picture of the Queen to remind you of home."

"Exactly," shouts the drunk. "You understand, Christiania is not Denmark, but we are still Danes and we love our Queen. Sven, two shots of vodka." He slaps a fifty kroner note down on the bar.

Once Sven has splashed two shots of vodka out in large glasses the drunk picks them both up, hands one to me, turns and shouts out at the top of his voice, "To Queen Margrethe!"

From all over Woodstocks the drunks lift whatever they are drinking and yell, "Queen Margrethe!"

A lady falls down in the corner and doesn't get back up and I don't feel like I am too far behind her. That last vodka was the end of me. I turn to Lonni and try to tell her that I need to go home, but the words come out as a grunt. "You need to go home," she says seeing my state of near incapacitation. All I can do is nod and even that doesn't happen as I mean it to, my head just lolls from side to side.

THE THREAT

After devouring bacon and eggs at the Moonfisher and finally getting past the worst of my hangover, I'm back at Kalle's preparing the soil at the side of his house, although I am facing a problem with Tina, the dog. Kalle gave me clear instructions not to disrupt her as she is so very old, but over half her day is spent lying in a shallow hollow in the middle of the patch where Kalle wants his grass. I've levelled it out as best I can but Tina's spot is right in the middle. I stand in the sun, stripped to my shorts and covered in dirt, wondering how to solve the problem. Tina can't see or hear well so the only way to get her to move is to physically push her away and if I did Kalle would not be happy. He will have to decide if he wants a dog-sized hollow in the middle of his grass or deny Tina her afternoon snoozing spot. I knock on his front door and he yells out to enter.

In Kalle's loungeroom there are two massive men with enormous bellies and tattoos down the length of their arms and up the back of their thick necks. Kalle has short cropped hair, but both these guys have long braided ponytails that reach well into the smalls of their back. One of the men has the word Angel tattooed down his forearm and I am sure that his shirt's sleeve hides the word Hell's. While they both look like bikers, neither have the Hell's Angels patch on their jacket. Again, the proudest of the proud hide their allegiance while in Christiania. There is a moment's pause before Kalle says, "I'm glad you came in." he reaches behind the couch. "I want you to meet a friend of mine."

From behind the couch he pulls a shotgun with a barrel so thick I could stick my thumb down it. Kalle lays the shotgun across his lap and strokes it as though it is a cat. "Meet my friend, Smith and Wesson." He stares at me harshly and we hold each others gaze.

The bikers lean back into the couch and wait to see how I will react. I am not sure what is going on or why Kalle has pulled this shotgun out on me. Obviously he is sending me a message, but I am unsure of its meaning. The naivety must be evident on my face as Kalle leans forwards and continues, "You don't see these gentlemen, they were never here. When you are in this house you never see anything." Kalle pumps a cartridge into the breach of the shotgun with loud click-clack. "Do you?"

"Not a thing," I say, finally catching on to the point of the shotgun and feeling especially glad that I have come to see him about the old dog Tina rather than just push her aside. "Tina keeps lying on the grass patch and I don't want to move her without talking to you about it first."

Upon hearing his dog's name Kalle's expression is immediately touched by love and his voice softens. "Tina is old. Just let her be, do the best you can to work around her. Now, go, fuck off and get back to work," he adds while returning the shotgun to its place behind the couch. "Oh, before you go," he yells out as I am about to walk out the door.

He doesn't say anything more, but throws me a block of hash.

The rest of the morning I work around Tina, she really is quite beautiful in her old age.

HELL'S ANGELS

I work in a gang of four building a fence around the Moonfisher's beautiful grass glade. One of the guys, Juan, is from Mexico and is sending the money he earns home to his family while he sleeps on the streets out in the city. He teaches me how to stay warm during cold nights by wrapping newspaper around my body under a leather jacket. He tells me this as we dig holes together for the fence posts. Axel has us painting the bottom of the posts with tar and copper paint so they won't rot. "They won't be able to kick this fence down in the future," he says angrily, referring to those Christianites who don't believe in borders of exclusion and continue in their attempts to kick our fence down.

Axel has developed quite an obsession with building the strongest fence possible. The joints where the fencing boards attach to the fence posts are extremely strong, held together with carved joints and thick nails. "Build it strong boys," he says to us. "Let them break their feet when they try to kick it down!"

We laugh at him, but we too want to build a lasting fence as our own mark on Christiania and the runestone that sits in the middle of the park.

I'm working hard, sweating with my shirt off and my hair coated in dirt, sticking to the skin on my shoulders. Throughout the morning I have noticed the blonde from Detlif's party, Erik the Viking's girlfriend, or rather ex-girlfriend, sitting on a bench and leaning back against the Moonfisher's wall. She's watching me. Every so often we catch each other's eye.

When I've finished the afternoon's work I gather up the tools and carry them back towards the Moonfisher. As I approach, sweating and covered from head to toe in a fine film of dust, she stands and walks over to intercept me. "Hi," she says, "my name is Nancy. Here I've written it down so as you don't forget it." She hands me a small scrap of paper with her name written on it.

"Hi," is all I can say back to her, before I blurt, "I have to pack the tools away." I walk off chastising myself for failing to continue the conversation that she was so obviously keen to start.

While I'm packing the tools away in a shed, all the people at the Moonfisher, including the staff, run out into the park and off towards Pusher Street. Lunar, one of the Moonfisher crew, is jogging past and I yell out to her, "What's happening?"

"Just come, follow me," she yells over her shoulder with an air of desperation.

I can't see any reason for panic, but everyone else certainly does. People from everywhere are running towards the bottom of Pusher Street near the Woodstock Bar. I run after Lunar who by now is sprinting with her long hair flowing out behind her. She leads me, as a part of a large group following her, to two huge men standing around at the entrance to Grøntsagen. With muscular arms covered with tattoos and long hair plaited into pony tails they are bikers for sure. Unlike the other Hell's Angels I have met and seen in Christiania they are actually wearing their patch insignia's on their leather jackets. The words: Hells Angel's, arch boldly across the back of their leathers, with Denmark, M.C. across the bottom.

"Take it off," yells Lunar, aggressively to one of the men.

"What off?" snarls the larger of the two Angels.

"Your jacket," Lunar snarls back like a crazed junk yard dog. "No patches in Christiania!"

"Like fuck I'm taking it off!"

"Then get the fuck out," Lunar shouts back raising her arm to point down Pusher Street and the city beyond.

While Lunar is a strong girl, she certainly is no Hell's Angel. I've never seen anyone speak to the Hell's Angels like this before.

"Fuck off!" shouts Lunar again.

The Angels themselves are gobsmacked. They can't seem to believe what they're hearing. The less massive of the two takes a menacing step towards Lunar and inflates his chest, but before he can complete the step Lunar has also moved forward and gets right up into his face. This stuns the Angel, obviously not used to a woman countering his aggression. "What are you going to do?" she taunts him, and the Angel is starting to notice the crowd that has gathered around. Two to three hundred people crowd up and down the street. For the first time, the bikers' appear a little anxious. The crowd has encircled them and quietly lends their collective power to Lunar who is still moving forward, closing the gap between herself and one of the Angels. They stand nose to nose, toe to toe. The Angel glances from side to side surveying the crowd, and sneers, "We don't take our patches off for anyone, we're the Hell's Angels!"

"Then as I said," Lunar lowers her voice to an almost inaudible whisper. "Get the fuck out!"

The crowd is hushed, closing the circle around the two Angels until it almost engulfs them completely. The Angels' slip from aggression and threat to fear and submission. These two huge biker outlaws are no match for the hundreds of people who surround them and they know it. While Lunar holds their gaze the bikers drop their shoulders, sliding their leather jackets down their arms and off their backs. They fold the jackets with great care and ceremony and hang them over their forearms, folding them inside out so the Hells Angels patches can't be seen. With her aggression tamed and arms folded, Lunar says, "Okay, but if we see those patches on you we will kick you out." She points down Pusher Street towards the city and with a final glare she turns and walks back towards the Moonfisher.

Now Lunar has gone the eyes in the crowd that only a moment before where spitefully glaring at the Angels quickly divert. After all, these two men standing in close proximity are still Hell's Angels and are known to be dangerous. Without their patches they appear no less menacing. The crowd disperses and I'm astonished.

I run back towards the Moonfisher trying to catch up to Lunar and reach her as she passes the runestone in the park. "Lunar. Lunar."

She turns, her hands trembling with adrenaline.

"Are you a mother?"

"Yes," she smiles. "I'm a mother."

GARBO

This morning I wait at the Machine Hall for my first garbage run. In true Christiania fashion all the guys who collectively run the place are late. They finally arrive and we climb the groaning, swaying staircase up to the loft office. Despite the late hour we sit down around a table for half an hour drinking coffee and smoking joints. Eric is big and broad with a large belly and crazy long curly black hair that makes him look like a pirate. He has one lazy eye that peers off into the corner of the room from time to time. Another of the collective, Kevin from England, introduces himself and explains that he and a couple of the Machine Hall guys are in a band. Kevin is completely bald with big bushy eyebrows and a small goatee beard on the underside of his chin. His round face and short, slightly stocky frame give him the appearance of a teddy bear. I've seen him playing an upright base in bands around Christiania a couple of times, the bulky base standing before him with the tuning keys high above his head. Today Kevin will take me to collect glass bottles and cardboard from around Christiania for recycling. "About four hours of towing a big trailer behind a tractor all over the Chrsitiania," he explains. "Picking up the recyclables then bringing it all back to the Machine Hall. A city truck will come and take it from there."

As Kevin and I leave the Machine Hall the sun has decided briefly to show us its form. All morning it has oscillated between rain and shine. The trailer is parked parallel to the Machine Hall. It is almost fifteen meters in length and constructed from old but sturdy wood and iron. Inside the Machine Hall, Kevin is getting a seventy-year old German tractor started to tow the hulking trailer. It is a very small tractor that slowly goes "bang, bang, bang," with all the power that one cylinder can muster. The seat is a single piece of flat iron that curves up from the chassis to provide some sort of comfort to the driver. With a little difficulty, Kevin and I hook up the trailer and, after placing some crates on its thick boards, are ready to go. Kevin guns the tiny engine with a hand operated throttle. I sit up behind him on one of the mudguards.

We chug past all the brightly graffitied buildings on the way down to Dussen where Lonni's place is, way out in the woods at the end of the lake. As we drive we have to shout over the engine noise. We drive all the way to the Kosmic Bloomst, the last building on the edge of Christiania. Kevin turns the little old tractor around and we begin picking up bottles that have been left out in front of people's homes. A few homes into the run Kevin jumps off the tractor. He buries the top half of his body in a garbage bin and pulls something out. "Hey, check this out."

I walk over to see that he is holding a green metal tube with a pistol grip.

"Do you know what it is?" he asks, handing me the tube.

At first I don't, but on its side *Danish Army* is written in black stenciled letters and I recognize it as tube used for launching rockets.

It takes a couple of hours to slowly make our way back to the village centre, where we bump into the Machine Hall Shit Sucking team and their tractor that is hooked up to a huge tank of festering shit. We all take a break for a joint and coffee at the Moonfisher Cafe.

I start talking to Michael, a guy I met at Detlif's party a couple of weeks ago. He is relaxed and happy, but tired and taking coffee to give him a boost for his day ahead counselling drug addicts out in the city. "Not really counselling," he says. "Giving them something stable and reliable in life when they have just come off the junk. Letting them know that someone cares for them."

The guys from the Machine Hall are at a nearby table talking music and rolling a joint. We are all dressed in shabby blue overalls. The break does not last long and I soon find myself perched back up on the tractor behind Kevin, who obviously loves driving the slow old German tractor through the dusty streets of Christiania. "I usually drive the other tractor," says Kevin. "But it is being used to suck shit today. This is the first time I've driven the one piston powered pony and I love her." He pats the tractor on the side like he is stroking the neck of a horse. "Yeah, she goes well," he keeps saying over and over above the bang, bang of its lonely but apparently happy piston.

Kevin and I collect a massive stack of beer bottles from the village centre then move onto the Bathhouse, the Green Hall, Nemoland, Woodstocks and the Lobben nightclub. Towards the end of the run Kevin lets me drive the old tractor. It's a perfect day perched on a tractor in the sun with the wind in my hair and diesel fumes up my nose. She is a breeze to drive, brake with the right foot on a metal rod, clutch with the left hand and throttle with the right using a lever by my knee. I get so confident that I reverse down the street and jackknife the trailer up onto some grass by the side of the road.

JUNK BLOCKAID

I laze back in a chair at the Moonfisher with my feet kicked forward, resting a hand on a glass of hot tea. Lunar is also at the table, she looks as though her day has been long and hard, but she is smiling. "Fuck man," she says. "It is good here now."

"It's great," I respond, thinking how correct her statement is.

"It's as though things are working, people are excited and confident. Do you know some people are starting a farm in the country to supply food for Christiania?"

"I'm surprised how active things are in Christiania, most people seem to be doing something. I love the homes people have built for themselves."

Lunar leans back in her chair. "People are proud, I like it, much better than before."

"Before?" I question, remembering what the old Hell's Angel I met on my first night had told me about biker wars and bodies buried in concrete.

"Yeah, before it was horrible," her face contorts as she spits the words out. "Man, there where junkies everywhere, and needles and people dying and freaking out. It was the fault of the fucking police."

"How was it the police's fault?"

"In the past, every time the police picked up a junkie out in the city they would say, "If you want to do this shit then go do it in Christiania", so all the junkies thought they would just squat here and they would shit and die in the buildings and fuck things up for the rest of us. Before we knew it there was junk everywhere."

Lunar is silent for a while. Talking about how Christiania used to be seems to have brought her down. After a moment's pause she continues. "I was only young at the time, living at the Children's House with all the other street kids of Christiania, no adults telling us what to do, but it was scary with all the junkies around and the bikers. Not like it is now, not at all."

I take a sip of my tea and ask, "What happened, how did it get better?"

"You haven't heard of the Junk Blockade?" Lunar asks, surprised.

"No, I'd never heard of Christiania until a few months ago."

Lunar lets out a short sigh. "When all the junkies were here shooting smack into their arms it was just terrible and we could see that it was ruining Christiania. We didn't know what to do and, as last resort, we decided to work with the police to get rid of the junkies and the heroin dealers. Some people from Christiania gave the police a list of the dealers who were selling heroin, they were mainly bikers. The police came into Christiania, hundreds of them, but they didn't bust the heroin dealers, they left them alone. Instead they rounded up and busted all the hash dealers, fucking pigs. We had made a deal with the police that we would help them get rid of the heroin, but they weren't supposed to touch the hash pushers. What's more the police gave the heroin dealers the names of the people who provided them the list. After that we couldn't trust the police and we had to deal with the junk problem ourselves, so, that's when the Junk Blockade happened. People in Christiania, you know, the community, mums and dads and kids even, went around to all the junkies and told them that they either get the fuck out of Christiania or go into rehab. It was mainly the mothers who drove it all, getting right up into the faces of the heroin dealers and making them leave. Day after day people went around Christiania confronting the junkies and heroin dealers and, over time, forced the junkies into rehab and the bikers out of Christiania. Put simply, a bunch of dickhead macho bikers were no match for mothers who didn't want their children to grow up among shit. The mothers of Christiania ended up being more ferocious and determined than either the junkies or the bikers. It is good now, the Moonfisher is moving forward. Our meetings are becoming more productive, people are serious. We're building this fence, laying the runestone. I'm feeling more confident too, feeling good." She smiles across to me.

I too am smiling. "I really never would have thought a place like Christiania could exist. Where I grew up everything was controlled by the government and big business and people would call you stupid if you ever suggested there was any other way of living."

"Fuck the government, fuck the straight world," says Lunar. Neither the government nor the straight world can touch her within Christiania.

"Hey, there is a party tonight, just on the other side of the park, near the Green Hall. "Come and have a beer."

I am still exhausted from the day's work, covered in dirt and stinking of dried sweat and smoke, but the idea of a beer is appealing. I'm enjoying Lunar's easy company, so I follow her across to the party.

Beers, two in a row and now sitting on my third, without any dinner and the world is a little less stable although far more relaxing. The music jives James Brown mashed with thumping beats and the dancing is wild. I've lost Lunar among the crowd and I'm in my own little party world in the darkness as others dance around me, strangers, but comrades, smiles and jives and good times. Next to me is a girl, she's moving her hips in time to the music, lifting her arms up to swipe her blonde hair from side to side. I try not to stare, but am mesmerized, finding it impossible to remove my eyes from her. I notice her watching me, watching her and realise, shocked, that it is for me that she moves her hips. She dances closer, daring and confident; close enough that I can smell her musky perfume. She slowly reaches out her arm, timing her movements to the music, grabs a handful of hair at the back of my head, pulling my face down to hers. I flinch, startled, not used to such force by a woman, she is taking what she wants and I feel unsure if I am willing to surrender it. She tightens her fist, pulling my hair, causing pain, but it only serves to further excite me. I cease resisting and allow my mouth to be pulled onto hers until our lips are sucking and biting. The party continues around us, inches away, dancing in the darkness to the wild beats.

She hooks a finger inside my shirt, dragging me to the side of the Green Hall, away from the dancers, deeper into the darkness and leans back against the wall. Pulling me on to her our bodies are pressed together. Again, I challenge my desires, this woman is like no other, I want her, but is it meant to be like this? I don't know her name, we haven't spoken single word!

She's kissing me deeply and squeezing a handful of my rump. Without conscious instruction, my hand searches out her breasts and slides across erect nipples under the soft fabric of her shirt. She groans, the first sound I hear from her. I kiss her neck, inhale her scent. She grinds her groin over my legs, gasping, pulling me closer, sliding her hand down my waist to rub my crotch. Just as I think she is about to undo my pants she hooks a finger over my belt, pulls away, issues an evil little grin and drags me, by the pants, through Pusher Street towards Christiania's main gate. I open my mouth, wanting to ask her name, but she places a finger to my lips and drags me into the back seat of a taxi. As she leans forward to whisper directions to the driver she places my hand between her legs, squeezing it between her thighs. With her head on my shoulder and her hand resting in my lap we drive away from Christiania.

Kissing and stumbling up several flights of stairs to her apartment, I am pushed onto her bed. Never before have I known such a woman, like a blood thirsty carnivore who tosses me about like a piece of raw meat. It feels somehow wrong, improper, but exhilarating. Having undone my jeans she feverously pulls them down, irritated when they catch on my ankles, but they are finally ripped off and flung to the far side of the room. She takes a firm hold of my cock begins to stroke it with one hand as she slips her shoes and pants off with the other. She lets go only long enough to whip the rest of her clothes over her head. As she climbs onto the bed she lowers her face to my groin and flicks her tongue out across the tip of my cock and issues another of her evil little grins. Our eyes lock together as she allows a thick line of saliva to fall from her tongue and over the head of my cock, rubbing it over my length, making it glisten, making it ready. She kneels over me, a leg either side of my hips, and begins to rub the head of my cock through her pussy, from the edge of her anus, between moist lips, issuing a soft groan each time I brush over her clitoris. With agonizing slowness she rubs back and forth allowing me a little deeper with each passing. I grasp her hips, pulling her down, attempting to penetrate her, but the strength in her legs is too much and she remains poised, hovering over me, sliding me through her wetness. Again, that evil little grin, teasing, knowing that I desperately want her to sink down on me, but she's in control and continues to slide her over me; denying me, teasing me. I'm tormented, tortured, the desire too much and I thrust my hips up into her. She groans, but lifts herself higher and I slip back out to be again teased against her clitoris. I release her hips and hold my forehead, unable to stand the torment, having no choice but to submit to her power. And just as I have chosen to submit, she slides her weight down the length of my shaft, burying me deep within her, tossing her head back, thrusting out her small breast, groaning. We stay motionless, tense, fully penetrated, the teasing over. She slumps her head forward, then her shoulders and her breasts fall over my face where I can suck at her erect nipples while she grinds ever deeper. Holding her hips I aid her thrusts, back and forth, as nipples flick in and out of my open mouth and across my tongue. Faster and faster we grind until the position serves no longer and she is again sitting up arching her back, holding an arm against the wall for balance, fucking me as hard as she can, thrusting her hips back and forth. Her mouth gapes wide, eyes close, poising to scream, but the only sound is our rubbing loins, wet in motion. Her shoulders shudder, coordination fails and she cums, eyes squeezed tightly, losing the rhythm, issuing a guttural groan, contorting her face as though in agonizing pain. Holding her by the nape of the neck, pulling her face into the pillow, I thrust my hips deep into her, pounding, slapping our skin together.

She pulls back, lifts herself off me and, without pause, runs her hair over down my stomach until her lips are wrapped around me. With hand and warm mouth she strokes and sucks until all the muscles in my body tense, pointed toes, rigid back and I explode over her lips and across her cheek. She continues to stroke, licking away at the glistening wetness, taking my entire length into her mouth, smiling at what she has achieved.

We lay in each other's arms, sweating, and finally I meet Mai. Her name is not actually Mai, but it takes one of those deep throated guttural Danish sounds to pronounce her name correctly, which I find impossible, so she tells me that Mai is just fine. She is a theology student at university. Her family doesn't live in Copenhagen so they help her rent this small apartment. It is tiny, with only a small kitchen and no bathroom or toilet. Besides studying theology, which seems a strange subject for someone as vivacious and wild as Mai has just proven to be, she is also an artist, a painter. She has a little studio room in the basement near the one shower and toilet that the whole building shares.

We go down to the basement to take a shower and then she shows me her paintings. Mai describes her style as big scribbles with a black marker pen on a large canvas, slowly filling in the spaces with shades of oil paints until the painting begins to emerge. "I don't really know what I'm painting until I see something within the scribbles then gradually the image takes form until the painting tells me what I'm painting, if that makes sense?"

It does.

The one currently on her easel is of a horse, defined by key angles and stokes among a swirling background of scribble. The horse is rearing and a ghostly character lurks under a mass of swirls that resemble a tree. It is emotive and descriptive without truly defining any of its content.

PALLE

Shit, I missed it, and I'm really angry with myself. I knew that the runestone dedication ceremony was to be conducted tonight, but I guess the beautiful heat of the sauna held me longer in its embrace than I intended and now I've missed the ceremony. It is dark in the Moonfisher's park with just a small fire burning. Erik, who has spent the last couple of months carving the runestone, is wearing a sheepskin vest and calf high boots, dressed up like a Viking with his golden hair in long plaits and thick leather bands covering his forearms. He has a beer in hand and appears elated in his conversation with a small group of people standing around the runestone. Palle, the old poet who wrote the poem that Erik carved onto the runestone, is dressed in a Viking druid's garb that includes a big pointy hat, like a wizard's, and a hessian smock tied with a thick piece of old rope around his huge belly. His wild and matted beard suits the druid's garb perfectly and between him and Erik I can easily imagine that it is a thousand years ago, in the old times as Erik would say. There is a bit of a party going on closer to the Moonfisher with good cheer and clinking bottles, but I make my way over to Palle who is sitting alone next to the fire. I don't really know Palle, but we have nodded to each other a few times in greeting while I was building the fence.

As I approach, Palle gestures a welcome and invites me to sit by him on a rock.

"You missed the ceremony," he says not taking his eyes off of the fire.

"I know," I sigh. "I'm angry at myself for missing it."

He looks over. "The ceremony was the first of its kind in a thousand years. It was very special."

Once again the magnitude of the runestone strikes home to me and I keep looking at Palle, the man who has signalled the return of the old ways through the dedication of the runestone. Even though I can sense his disappointment, Palle is warm towards me and in a soft gentle voice he says, "I see you write, I've seen you in the Moonfisher writing away by yourself while everyone plays pool and talks around you. What do you write?" The old poet looks at me in such a way that I feel it safe to convey to him what I would never tell anyone else.

"Just about Christiania really, the people, the place, what's happening. It's not really writing, just a whole lot of bullshit really."

"That's okay," says Palle with a knowing smile. "Some of the best writing is just a load of bullshit. Take Charles Bukowski for example. He lived bullshit, talked bullshit and wrote bullshit."

"Yeah, I don't drink like Bukowski though. I could never understand how he could write when he was so drunk. When I get that drunk I can't function, let alone write."

"Practice, practice," Palle says and hands me a beer.

Sitting with Palle, by the fire, an old poet and a young man, I feel like a writer for the first time in my life and we talk about writing and writers well into the early morning.

RENDEVOUS

Life is cluttered and cramped under Kalle's house in his small junk room. Among the junk is just enough room for an old bed with a fairly decent mattress on it. I have procured a bed sheet and pillow and am able to wash my cloths in a coin-operated laundry near an old run-down building called The Kitchen on Pusher Street. Daily trips to the Bathhouse keep me clean, while bacon and eggs from the Moonfisher, falafels from a stall up on Pusher Street and samousas, fruit and hard as nails bread rolls from Grøntsagen keep me sustained. There's not much room for life inside of Kalle's junk room but outside is a different picture. From the door of my room it is only two metres to the wide canal that runs the entire length of Dussen. The bank on the other side of the canal is thick with trees and green foliage. The canal forms one border of Christiania and divides it from the city on the other side, although you wouldn't know there was a city on the other side of the canal. The land disappears in the density of the forest that appears to stretch out forever on the far bank, but which is only about twenty metres deep before the concrete and bitumen of the city reclaim the ground.

    Each morning while I sit smoking on an old beer crate, I soak in the wall of nature that exists on the other side of the canal. Sometimes a goose will come in to land on the canal right in front of me with great wings arched high like parachutes. Its big webbed feet splashing great jets of water before it quickly slows and becomes a stable, gently bobbing, beauty with fine white feathers and an elegantly long neck.

    Most mornings, shortly after I awake, Tina the dog, makes her slow, limping, commute past my room from her early morning sun spot to her midday sun spot on the lawn I am trying to grow. She walks across the newly turned, raked and planted earth and settles herself down in the slight shallow, snoozing until the sun arcs behind a large tree late in the afternoon when she can once again catch the sun on Kalle's front porch.

    I sit on the upturned wooden beer crate leaning back against the house, listening to Kalle banging away up above in his kitchen. His footfalls send small vibrations through the house and into my back. I rarely hear him as he's often out of town and if he isn't he parties and stays out all night. Kalle lives alone, but I know that he has an ex-wife as I have once seen her come to the house. She didn't go inside, just stood out the front and yelled abuse at him, threw her handbag at his porch and left. I've seen lots of other women come and go at night, but they never stay long, and a few times I've seen the Hells Angels, without their patches. Mostly Kalle spends time on his own while he's in Christiania. It's his haven from a crazy outlaw lifestyle.

From around the corner of the house I hear rocks and gravel being pushed down the slope by sliding shoes and shortly Kalle pokes his head around the corner. "Hi, hi," he says, holding a hand up to shield his eyes from the sun.

He looks a little worse for wear after another late night partying, and I would think that with his hangover he would much prefer to still be in bed. However, Kalle has an energy that seems to propel him eternally onwards. Even in his groggy state his muscles twitch and bulge with his every movement. "I have a little girl," he says to me. And I want her to want to come and spend time with me."

He looks at me seriously and I guess he is trying to make me understand how important his little girl is to him.

"So, I want you to build me a beach for her to play on."

"A beach!" I laugh.

"Yes on this canal," and he turns to the canal and takes a moment to behold the beauty of it. "I want a beach for my little girl to come and play on. Can you do it?"

"Ahhhhh," is all I can say for a good ten seconds as I try to process the design and construction of a beach. I come up with a blank, but nonetheless say, "Sure I can, it'll just take a little while."

"Good, that's good," smiles Kalle. "I want my little girl to be happy here."

"I'll need to buy some materials though," I say, having no idea what they will actually be.

"Sure, just come and see me when you need money. Come have breakfast with me and then I need you to clean my boat." Kalle says slapping me on the back and leading the way up the steep, slippery slope at the side of his house. "Oh, I need you to build me some stairs here also."

"Okay," I smile as I grapple up the slope to the front of Kalle's house.

After breakfast we walk through Christiania, picking up one of Kalle's friends along the way. Approaching Pusher Street I notice the pushers registering that Kalle is among them. Most stand up or sit a little straighter, a little prouder. A few call out greetings while others simply wait until Kalle catches their eye and then offer a little nod of respect.

Outside Christiania's main gate we stand on the street curb and are faced with the five story canyon that is the inner guts of most big cities. Kalle hails a cab and it twists through busy streets, depositing us at a canal beside a long, sleek speedboat that has full apartment-style accommodation in its nose and massive couches at its stern. The fact that it is my job to wash it doesn't detract from my excitement, as I've never spent much time on boats. The idea of this one cruising through Copenhagen's canals on this one appeals greatly. However, it does take me several hours to clean and of course Kalle has other things to do, so he leaves me alone on the boat to wash and scrub. When he comes back the boat is immaculate. "Yeeeeha," he yells like a cowboy and leaps into the cockpit to fire up the boat's twin V8 engines.

The water churns at the stern and the whole boat vibrates, throbbing with the massive power of the engines. Kalle directs me through the casting off procedures and we quickly find ourselves motoring along the canal, which soon joins Copenhagen's narrow inner harbor. We follow the line of the big ships heading out to sea. I stand and salute the sailors watching us from the deck of a huge naval warship. At the helm, Kalle has slowed the boat and, like a driver looking to find a hard-to-see-street, is craning his neck to look down the canals that branch off Copenhagen's inner harbor. After drifting past a couple of narrow canals he recognises something and powers up slightly to enter one. This canal is lined with restaurants and cafes and designer clothes shops. Ferraris and Austen Martins are parked along the water's edge. Kalle is on his phone as we idle to a standstill, effectively double-parked next to an old, immaculately maintained wooden day boat. An old couple are having lunch on its deck. Kalle smiles at the oldies and gives them a wave. They stop chewing their lunch and stare, wondering why this tattooed, shirtless, muscle-bound hoodlum has stopped his great gurgling speedboat next to them. For an answer a dirty great big boot lands on the bow of their boat, violently rocking it, and from dry land steps the biggest, filthiest, longest haired, most tattooed Hells Angel that walks the face of the earth. And as we are outside of Christiania, this one is wearing the Angels patch on the back of his leather wastecoat. The sheer weight of the Angel rocks the old couple's day boat with each well placed step he takes. When the old couple see what is walking across the deck of their boat they become motionless as though they do not want to provoke a wild animal. I am sure that they did not expect this in what is obviously one of the more exclusively wealthy areas of Copenhagen.

With the Angel onboard the boat, Kalle gives another wave to the old couple and once more flashes his charming smile. The boat drifts out into the canal under the momentum generated by the Angel jumping on board and Kalle engages the engines to produce an almighty roar that lifts the boat's nose high into the air. We tear down the canal sending a rolling wake across the narrow width of water that slaps into the wall and sends a salty spray over a number of luxury sports cars.

Passing out of the inner harbor, Kalle fully lets fly. The boat stands even higher in the water and starts shooting jets of spray out each side of the bow every time we smash into a peak in the swell. Racing away from Copenhagen and into the straight that separates Denmark and Sweden the swell picks up and the boat jars as it slaps harder and harder against the rolling water. We experience the jarring of sudden deceleration as we hit each wave and then accelerate quickly as the boat smashes its way through to the next one. The four of us on board hold on tight as though we are riding a bucking bull determined to throw us into the inky green sea.

Soon it becomes evident that Kalle is aiming the boat towards a small island sitting roughly halfway between Sweden and Denmark. It has small rocky cliff faces and what appear to be concrete bunkers sitting on the bluffs. A jetty juts out from one side of the island surrounded by a couple of buildings. Approaching the jetty Kalle barks out orders for the docking procedure. Although it is my first time on a boat and my sum total experience consists of casting off and cleaning, I follow his instructions and feel like a pro as I swing a salt-encrusted loop of rope around an iron bollard at the jetty's end.

On the island, Kalle tells me to go for a walk up to one of the bluffs while he and the Angel walk off in another direction. I'm keen to explore the concrete defensive bunkers on the island, no doubt a relic from World War II. I find tunnels through the island that are long and dark. In places they are pitch black and my footfalls echo loudly. I wander through them trailing my hand along their walls to find my way through the darkness. Their surfaces are rough with trickles of water and the thick smell of mould. A spiral stairwell carved into the rock leads up to rusted steel gun emplacement that overlooks the approach to the channel of water. It is an overcast day and the wind blows strongly. I spy Kalle and the Angel down on a small stony beach. They see me too and Kalle waves and points to the restaurant by the jetty, signaling that I should join them there.

At the restaurant the others are talking in Danish so I take out my notepad and start to write. The Angel watches me write and looks at Kalle sternly, grumbling something in Danish. Kalle laughs as he glances sideways at me and says to the Angel, "It's okay, he's met my friends Smith and Wesson."

The Angel doesn't seem impressed but thankfully appears satisfied, although he stills glares at me and the message he is communicating is clear: don't fuck with me. He leans back in his chair and reverts to ignoring me again. Just like a Don in a Godfather movie, Kalle lavishly orders food for us all and we settle in for a long lunch, devouring a mountain of food. With coffee on the way Kalle takes out a giant block of hash and rolls a foot long joint. About to light it, the oldest of the waiters, perhaps the owner, steps over to our table and politely asks Kalle not to light the joint in his restaurant. As though he is the definition of a gentleman, Kalle charmingly apologises and tucks the joint away up the sleeve of his jacket. We smoke it on the way back to Copenhagen bouncing through the waves.

CULT, COMUNE, WHAT?

On my way back to the little junk room under Kalle's, the narrow dirt path takes me past a small gravel beach on the lake's edge. Earlier in the day I had seen a group of people building a fire on the beach. Now, walking in the night's blackness I can hear a low chanting. Unable to make out the mantra I can hear low primordial voices resonating in unison. As I come closer the light from the fire pokes through tiny holes in the wood's foliage and I'm able to discern the figures of a small group of people. They are holding hands facing the fire. Now I can hear their mantra clearly: "Weeeeee suuuurrreeeeeendeeeerrrrr ooooouuuuuurrrrrr ennnnnnnneeeeeeerrrrrrgieeeeeeeessssss, weeeee suuuuurrreeeeeendeeerrrr ooouuuuurrrrr ennnnneeeeergieeeees," over and over in trance.

    With almost one thousand people living in the Freetown outside of the confines of the straight world it wouldn't be hard for an outsider to label Christiania a cult or commune, especially if they could see this group holding hands and chanting around a fire. Generally, in the straight world when someone hears about a group of people living differently, as they are here in Christiania, they respond by saying something like, "Oh, I could never be a part of a cult," or "communes aren't for me." But the plain truth about Christiania is that it is neither a cult nor a commune. For the months I have lived here not a single person or group of people, including the Hell's Angels, have displayed any religious or theological influence over the rest of Christiania's community. There is no governing philosophy or ideology that offer any judgement on peoples' actions. And as far as a commune goes, nothing could be further from the truth. There is no central division of wealth or reallocation of goods. In fact, with the hash trade as its pinnacle, a vibrant capitalist economy flourishes with many and varied businesses and collectives feeding from it. Without doubt, the pushers are rich, but they mostly spend their money within Christiania, buying their food, their entertainment and their home renovations from the many and varied Free Town businesses. With an easily described self-sustained capitalist economy, Christiania could never be called a commune. It defies descriptions. The best the Danish government can come up with is that it is a social experiment, as though they had a hand in planning it, which of course they did not. I think most Christianite's prefer not to define it, it is what it is.

FLY LIKE A BUTTERFLY

Kalle is probably the best boss I have ever worked for. The most relaxed, for sure. I work whenever I feel like it. Miss a day, no problem. If the sun is shining I might simply wander off and do nothing, or perhaps I'll just get stoned and massacre waist-high weeds with an electric grass cutter or climb a tree and chop off its branches. His backyard has turned into my own private playground where I get filthy, stoned, destroy and create. At the end of each week, or more usually whenever I can track Kalle down, I get paid in cash from great wads that he pulls from his pocket. I can hardly believe he is paying me to build a private beach in his backyard.

A beach? I ponder, as I sit out the back of Kalle's place on the beer crate. How can I possibly build a beach? Kalle also wants nice grass around the beach and a retaining rock wall, which involves cutting down another tree and burning its roots out. I'm thinking about building the beach by extending two triangles out over the water. Hopefully the triangles will give the illusion of the sand leading all the way to the water's edge. I can't make it a beach with water lapping right onto the sand for two reasons. First, it would be impossible to make an effective transition between the nice pristine sand and the dirty brown muck that is the canal bed. And second, I would not want to even dip my big toe into that canal water. I've heard that when the Danish military vacated Christiania a whole lot of ammunition was dumped into the canal and has resulted in heavy metal poisoning. Probably not something that Kalle would want his little daughter playing in either. I've been sketching a few designs in my notebook and while I haven't come up with the solution just yet, at least I have some confidence that I can actually build what I promised Kalle.

I work at Kalle's with my shirt off and a pair of denim shorts that used to be a pair of jeans. No shoes, as I love the dirt and mud squishing between my toes as I chainsaw trees down, dig out roots and burn a big fire under the tree stump. Soon I am covered in sweat and grimy dirt as flames lick up into the air and threaten to catch my knotted, clumped hair on fire, infusing it with smoke. Generally I finish working at Kalle's a few hours after midday when I head to the Bathhouse for more sweating and more mud-smeared action over my skin followed by an ice cold shower that pricks my senses and leaves me feeling fresh and exhilarated.

Then I usually go to the Moonfisher to sip hot tea and dangle long joints from the tips of my fingers. Not quite so long as the local's masterpieces, but I'm getting there. The hot sauna relaxes the strain in my muscles, its oppressive heat lending a veil of relaxation, the Moroccan mud leaves my skin baby smooth.

Today a young woman keeps looking my way. She started off glancing at me and then looking away when I caught her gaze, but now she simply stares and it is more than a little disconcerting. She is small with a round face and tight ringlets through her hair. A deep furrow runs across her brow in a thick crease. As I roll my second joint for the evening she comes and sits at my table with a wanton look in her eyes, "Can I share that with you?" She's Italian, I can tell by the way she bounces her words and favors her vowels. I've met a quite a few Italians over the years and each time my belief that all Italians are crazy is enhanced. I wonder if this girl will lend weight to such a theory. "I'm an artist," she says. "A photographer and painter."

I hadn't asked her, but like most Italians she wants to tell me about herself and seems uncomfortable in silence. "But I'm also an angel, a beautiful angel, can't you see!"

I can't, but not wanting to offend, say, "Of course you are."

"I am a homeless angel, a free angle. I was living in the city, but my flatmate kicked me out. I don't like her."

"I wouldn't either."

"You know I could turn you into a butterfly," she says. "I could have you flapping your wings." And with a cheeky gleam in her eyes and wry smile I can tell exactly what she is meaning.

I light the joint and pass it across to her. She takes a long toke and continues talking about her art, only slightly making sense. Like other Italians I know she holds onto the joint like it is a microphone, talking, talking, puff, talking, talking.

"You know that is a boomerang joint," I say to her.

"A what?" She has no idea what I'm talking about.

"Yeah, it comes back."

"Oh, sorry, I just lose myself so easily." And she finally hands the joint back to me.

I puff on it. While I have the joint she stops talking, staring at me with wide luminous eyes through which I can see the zing of intense energy. I toke again and pass it back to her. She immediately begins to talk again.

"My art is not art. I hate the art world, those fucking idiots caught up in their bullshit labels and critical judgment."

"What is your art? What do you do?"

"My art is shit," she says. "Literally. But they don't understand. It is kind of Dadaism, I take a photo of my shit and blow it up really big, can you imagine a six foot shit? Then I use acrylic paint to highlight the contours on it. Do you know how hard it is to do a really good shit worth taking a photo of? When I started I would just shit everywhere trying to get the background contrast right. I wouldn't shit for days trying to save it all up for one big shit worthy of a photo, but then I realised I didn't have to do that. After a while I worked out that I'd just have to eat the right foods. By experimenting I worked out that a meat only diet and no beer gave the best results. My fucking flatmate thinks she too is an artist, but she just doesn't understand."

"She didn't like you shitting everywhere?" I sympathise with her flatmate.

"No, she was okay with that. She was doing a series of work with piss in fine crystal, but she was a vegetarian and couldn't stand meat being in the refrigerator, fucking bitch!"

She passes the joint back to me and is silent once more while I take a few tokes and blow the smoke into the air over her head.

"So what's Dadaism? I don't know much about art."

"It's anti-art. Fuck art I say, and so too do the Dadaists. Those pricks at the university don't know what they're talking about."

"Anti art? I like it," I smile at her.

She appears to be encouraged, "Yes me too, it is my life. Dadaism kind of says that the art world is shit, metaphorically I mean. Dada says that art justifies or legitimizes the view of the masses and only serves to enforce the status quo. It says that art is just really beautifying the world, validating it. Dada embraces irrationality and chaos and is kind of like a protest against art. While art stands to recreate and justify the way life is Dadaism stands to reject it and break it down."

"Kind of like Christiania," I add

"Well sort of, yeah I guess it is, I hadn't thought about that. Like in here I am an angel and no one questions it, I'm accepted as an angel, but out there in the city I'm just a homeless freak who takes photos of my shit. I will stay with you tonight," she tells me.

And she does, transforming me into a butterfly until I flap my wings and drift to the ceiling of the small room under Kalle's house.

POLICE

I've seen large piles of paving stones at the end of Pusher Street, near the main gates of Christiania, and have decided to use them to build two small rock islands just off the bank of the canal at Kalle's place. Then I can lay four railway sleepers out to them to create two triangles with bases that stretch about twenty feet along the canal's shoreline. If I attach some boards to the bottom of the triangles I will then be able to fill it up with sand, making a big sandpit extended out over the water. The tips of the triangles will offer the illusion of the sand meeting the water in a beach-like style. I'll also use the discarded paving stones to build a rock retaining wall. I've finished cutting all the trees down and have burnt out their roots. The canvas is blank and now it is time to start creating.

The Machine Hall has a cart that I can use to drag the piles of paving stones about two kilometres across the lake and down through Dussen to Kalle's house. As I walk up through Dussen and over the lake I notice that someone is running a guided tour of Christiania. A group of about ten tourists, cameras swinging around their necks, are being led down past the big open windows of the Bathhouse. The tourists get a nice view of the shower stalls and their naked occupants washing mud off of their bodies. The tour guide stops by the windows and I can hear him telling the tourists about the Bathhouse and how important it is to Christiania. The tourists hardly know where to look. The owners of the bodies don't seem to mind and do nothing to hide themselves from the tourists' view.

Passing the Moonfisher I see the half-finished fence around the park and feel pleased that I am contributing to the building of the Free Town. I stop in at Grøntsagen to see Lonni and buy a pear and a samosa for lunch.

"Hi, Hi," I say to Lonni and she beams at me with a big grin. "Hey, I saw some of my own kind today. I feel so much better, not so homesick."

"What?" She has no idea what I'm talking about.

"Tourists! I saw a group of tourists down by the Bathhouse."

"Ooooo, I know," says Lonni with a smile. "It's so fuuuuny. It's Lupe, he's always taking the tourists to the Bathhouse to watch everyone showering. He gets in trouble for it, but I think it's fuuuunny. Hey, you going to the party tonight? It's the mid-summer solstice."

"Didn't know there was one, but you bet. Are you going?"

"I can't, I should stay home with the girls," says Lonni with a feigned sad look. "Whatchya doing?" She asks, poking me in the ribs.

"Nudding," I joke. "Really, getting a cart from the Machine Hall and grabbing some of those paving stones at the end of Pusher Street. I'm building a beach for Kalle!"

"A beach, but you can't take those stones, they won't let you."

"Who?"

"The pushers, they need them."

"What, for getting stoned?" I laugh.

"Nooooo," Lonni shushes me. "For when the police come. Did you say you're building a beach?"

"Yeah, for Kalle, I've also built him some stairs. Thanks heaps for linking me up with him."

"Sorry that you are sleeping in that little messy room," she says to me with regret in her voice.

"No, don't apologise, I love it. Man, the geese landing on the water, the cool evening breeze rustling all the leaves. It's a nice private, pretty little spot."

I sit with Lonni talking for a while. Every so often she has to get up to serve a customer. It's nice to be in her company, so exuberant and with such innocent excitement but also deep wisdom. The day is moving on though and I want to get a start on transporting those paving stones from Pusher Street down to Kalle's place. I figure that I am going to need quite a few cartloads to build the islands and retaining wall.

Leaving Grøntsagen I pass the front of Nemoland. It is mid-afternoon so the place is quite full with people supping beer and downing shots. I've noticed that while the Moonfisher doesn't usually serve beers, I rarely see people smoking joints at Nemoland. I'm not sure if it is by design but alcohol and ganja seem to have been separated in Christiania. There is plenty of both, but people tend to be in one camp or the other. The drinkers are generally found at either Nemoland or Woodstocks, while the smokers tend to gravitate to the Moonfisher café and Monsters.

Walking past the W.C. Fields Club I wave to Poo and Gunner and shout out, "Hi, hi." Turning the corner onto Pusher Street I weave my way through the throng of people buying hash at the pusher's tables. I walk the length of Pusher Street and into the Machine Hall where I yell up to curly hair, pirate Eric, in the loft office. "I'm taking the hand-cart."

"Right-O," he yells back unseen.

Eric offered the handcart to me for free this morning when I asked him how much it was to hire. The cart is basically a big steel frame with car wheels. Plyboard is laid across the top of the frame to carry a load and a steel beam with a crossbar juts out the front of the cart. It's pretty basic, but just what I need to haul a couple hundred pavers across the lake to Kalle's place. The cart clangs and jerks as I drag it out of the Machine Hall and over to the nearby pile of paving stones. The pavers have been pulled up and dumped in two piles at the end of Pusher Street. Maybe Lonni was right, the piles seem to be strategically placed a little more than a stone's throw away from Christiania's main gate. If ever the pushers needed to throw something at the police coming into Christiania the pavers are in the perfect location. The stones are old, smooth and worn. I guess they must have been part of the old military base's parade grounds. As I'm positioning the cart near one of the piles I notice a couple of the pushers looking at me as if to say, "Hey, what are you doing with our stones?"

The pushers at this end of Pusher Street are all big, tough looking guys. Even the smaller ones appear big as they strut in an aggressive way. Most are wearing singlets to show off their muscles and tattoos. Gold chains and gold teeth glint in the sun. Dogs lay at their feet with spiked collars and chain leads. I usually walk quickly past this end of the Pusher Street with my eyes cast down doing my best not to get in anyone's way. Yet here I am today taking their strategically placed, police defying ammunition. What am I doing?

I pick up a couple of stones and drop them onto the cart with a loud crash. I wince at the noise it makes as it only draws further attention to what I am doing. With the loud bangs of the stones landing onto the cart more of the pushers notice me, stealing their stones. None of them say anything, but I can tell that it is only a matter of time before one of them does and I'm wondering what to say to them when they do. Oh, crap, one of the pushers is coming over to me with his dog, chain in hand, muscles flexed and chest puffed out.

"What are you doing, hey?" he asks in a deep, aggressive voice, his shoulder and chest muscles bulging out from under his singlet. A big letter "T" hangs around his neck on a thick gold chain.

"Um, well, I'm building something for Kalle." I have a feeling that most of the big aggressive pushers at this end of Pusher Street know Kalle and I'm hoping his name saves me.

"Kalle eh, you work for Kalle?" he asks, not toning down his posture at all.

"Yeah, man, I'm doing something for Kalle."

The pusher is quite for a while, as though his thinking has stalled. During the pause there is a sudden shout: "Police!"

Everyone freezes. Even the dogs are still. We all turn our heads towards the main gates and see two policemen walking into Christiania. Within a heartbeat pandemonium breaks out all along Pusher Street. The pushers swipe their arms across their tables and tumble all their hash and grass into bags, pockets, boxes, anything available to simply get their stuff out of sight. The pushers sprint off down Pusher Street away from Christiania's main entrance. The two policemen slowly stroll into the Free Town. Dogs are barking and people are shouting and running while these two policemen are looking like they are simply going for a lunchtime stroll and a friendly chat. They don't appear to be the usual, young, cocky police. Instead they are quite old, grey haired and quite distinguished in their appearance. They seem to be taking their time surveying Pusher Street. I guess they are senior police commanders rather than rank and file.

I stand alone at the end of Pusher Street with these two senior policemen walking towards me. Pusher Street has emptied out like a Wild West movie and it would be fitting if a tumbleweed were to roll on by. Moments before it had been a frenzy of activity as people rushed to vacate, now there is an eerie silence. Perhaps I too should run, but I want to get some work done on the beach and I've done nothing wrong, have no reason to fear the police. Kalle's name might not have saved me from the aggressive pusher, but these police certainly have. I may be the only person in the whole of Christiania happy to see them right now. "Hi, hi," I say and offer a little wave to the two senior police as they approach, but they pretend to ignore me and act as though the job of looking around Pusher Street is much too important to be distracted from. They don't come far into Christiania, only thirty or forty metres down Pusher Street.

They point various things out to each other and write notes on small pads. I figure that I should make the most of the quite street to load up the cart with paving stones while the pushers aren't around. How pathetic they are, all big and tough with their pile of stones ready to throw and then they all run away like children at the sight of these two old cops. Clang, I throw a stone onto the cart, the only sound up and down an almost empty Pusher Street.

The police are still standing around by the time I've fully loaded the cart. It takes great effort to drag it all the way down to Kalle's place across the lake and I'm exhausted and covered in sweat by the time I get it there. I have just enough energy to unload the stones in a big pile out the back of Kalle's, return the cart to the Machine Hall and then collapse onto the wooden bench in the Bathhouse's sauna.

It's hard to say how long I sweat and laze in the sauna as time tends to warp in a haze of heat and steam. It might be twenty minutes or three hours, it doesn't matter. What matters is that I go into the Bathhouse tired and exhausted and emerge from it, sometime later, with a totally fresh, reinvigorated sense of being. I am starting to believe that saunas are simply the most amazing invention in the history of humankind and I thank the Scandinavians for them. It is early evening when I emerge from the Bathhouse and, being right next the Moonfisher, a cup of tea and joint is too difficult to pass up.

SUMMER SOLSTICE

I sit, alone, on a rock at the edge of the Moonfisher's park, blowing the steam off of a cup of tea and slowly rolling a joint. There is a larger than usual crowd at the Moonfisher tonight and the pre-emptive feeling of a party is growing in vibrancy as friends greet each other and stand around talking. Happy beats are played on the Moonfisher's outside speakers and the summer twilight gradually turns from the radiant glow of the day to the purple hue of night, never completely reaching blackness before the sun fully rises again in the morning. I see a few people I know and nod to them or wave when our eyes meet, but tonight I'm essentially alone. It would be good to sit here with Lonni, anticipating the party and making jokes, but she is looking after her girls. I have missed her company since moving into Kalle's junk room.

The crowd at the Moonfisher grows and soon the people are no longer just standing around. Feet are shuffling, knees are bending and arms swing back and forth in time to the beats. It was almost imperceptible, but the party has started. Someone drops a glass onto the concrete out the front of the Moonfisher and the crowd roars and jeers in good humor. Loud dance beats emanate from the direction of Christiania's soccer oval, the Meadow of Peace, over past Nemoland. The crowd at the Moonfisher slowly drifts towards it. From out of the crowd I see Mai, walking over to sit next to me. "Hello stranger."

It is the first time I've seen Mai since we fucked and I'm a little unsure as to how to act towards her. "Hi, hi," is all I say.

She seems to sense my unease and says, "It's okay, I'm not looking for a boyfriend, it was just some fun we had together."

We talk and joke together as the crowd at the Moonfisher continues to thin out in favor of the party that is booming not far away. It's nice sitting with Mai. She has an easy, quirky way about her and I quickly settle into her company. Mai has come to Christiania tonight for the party and we soon join the flow of people towards the Meadow of Peace, stopping at Nemoland for a few shots of tequila and some beers. By the time we reach the massive party we are mildly drunk and involuntarily bopping to the dance beats. A loud boom sounds, an explosion, and on the edge of the field a metal rubbish bin launches fifty metres into the air sailing in a slow arc and landing, harmlessly, on the outer edge of Christiania. Following the explosion the dancing intensifies and a seething mass of revellers fling arms into the air in worship to the homegrown pyrotechnics and the summer solstice.

I'm jabbing my arms in time to the techno, stomping my feet on the dewy grass and smiling like a crazed jackal. Not far from me Mai is doing the same, among four or five hundred others. The vibe is inclusionary and strangers become friends, pointing fingers at each other to command movements and energy. I quickly lose Mai to the crowd and find myself blissfully alone in the seething oneness that is the party, kicking out my legs, throwing out my arms to embrace the dharma, thrashing my hair, gnashing my teeth. As the parties energies sway back and forth through the crowd I direct my energies to those dancing with the music flowing through them and occasionally take the energies of others when the circle of energy holds me in its centre. The night becomes darker, but never black, just a deeper shade of purple as the Scandinavian sun dips to its lowest point of the night.

Hours later, it seems, I feel like smoking a joint. As I have no hash I walk past Nemoland and the W.C. Fields Clubhouse to Pusher Street, which is also in party mode. Strobe lights flash bright light up and down Pusher Street and people stand shoulder to shoulder among the pusher's stalls. People are hanging out of the windows on the second story of the buildings that line the north side of the street. It seems everyone is yelling and it is that particular point in a party when everyone appears crazed. I buy a small block of hash and sit in the gutter to roll my joint. The world, tonight, is filled with freaks. Space suits and fluorescent body paint, huge silly hats, a couple of clowns and even a Santa Claus. Everyone is smiling and saying, "Hi, hi," to strangers they bump into and I'm simply, stunningly, happy to just watch the world go by. And not just any normal straight world, but a world born of anarchy and freedom. No aggression, no straight world hang-ups, no police, just a massive throng of free people letting their hair down on the summer solstice.

Joint smoked and I'm happy wandering back towards the Meadow of Peace, past the bikers in Nemoland, past the W.C. Fields Club with Poo and Gunner, two old guys supping beers like it was any normal Monday morning for them and not a manic, raging, freakoid party. "Hi guys," I yell to them from a distance and they raise their bottles at me to toast the night. They grin at me as I'm more than a little wasted and my steps are wayward. Back on the Meadow of Peace among the partying freaks and I'm dancing, alone, yet with everyone. Before long I notice a tall, sexy blonde girl dancing next to me. It takes me a while to realize that's she is directing her energies towards me and I recognize her, not straight away though, to be Nancy, Erik the Viking's ex-girlfriend. She sees that I've finally recognised her and dances closer, ignoring all the other thousands of people and focusing her energy on me. If I was sober I know I would shy away from her bold attention, but tonight, the way I'm feeling, the way the crowd is making me feel, the way the summer solstice lunacy has infected me, I accept her energies and direct my own back towards her. Soon she is up close and touching me, no words, just movements. A slight caress to a beat, a touch to a tweet, and I'm returning the same. I touch her hips and she turns around and wraps my arm around her and across her breasts, small and firm with erect nipples that I can feel through the thin fabric. From behind I grab her hair in a gentle hold and pull her head back until it rests on my shoulder. I can smell her scent, a mixture of musky perfume, her sweat and pheromones. She reaches behind with her hand and grabs my trousers, forcing my hips onto hers and then I'm kissing her neck, smelling her hair, firmly holding her breasts. We separate and continue to stomp to the thumping beat with our eyes locked, smiling. Knowing that we have communicated a meaning with no words uttered. We dance for hours, sometimes apart staring at each other, sometimes holding each other, not kissing, just caressing and knowingly teasing ourselves. Time stands still. The party around us rages, but we are alone in each other's company, the crowd is simply a landscape. Not arms flaying to the beat, but branches in the wind, not hands thumping time, but fluttering foliage. We are alone in our forest, two intrepid explorers having found one another in this party.

Gradually, the purple night of midsummer is impinged by an increasing blue hue that announces the dawn. The forest of revellers gradually thins and my arms become heavy, my legs cease their willful stomping and Nancy and I realise our moment has come to the end. Without words she follows me away from the Meadow of Peace, past Nemoland, the Moonfisher, across the bridge and down the dirt road to

Kalle's house and my little, junk-filled room. Just as we are taking off our clothes there is a knock on the door. I open it, while Nancy jumps into my bed and out of sight, and see Mai standing before me. She accepts that I have another lover already warming my bed. Kissing me deeply, flicking her tongue into my mouth she pulls away and says, "Fuck her well lover, just like I showed you. I'll come see you another time." And she quickly walks away disappearing around the corner of Kalle's house.

From under the blanket Nancy looks at me and smiles as though she is the master and I the puppy about to be played with. I, however, have a different view of the situation and, inspired by Mai, rip the blanket off to reveal her nakedness. Nancy issues a squeal and instinctively places a hand over each breast. I lay beside her, propped up on an elbow and kiss her, softly at first, then deeper as our passion begins to take hold. With my free hand I run a finger down her breast bone, across her level stomach to the uppermost reaches of soft pubic hair and then back between her breasts, under her jaw and behind her ear, again, this time reaching further down through her pubic hair. Each time I trace my fingers down her body they reach further between her thighs gliding over her lips and back again, all the way to the nape of her neck. With each passing of my fingers Nancy's stomach muscles shudder and she arcs the small of her back, inviting my fingers to explore deeper, but as her hips push forward my hand draws back, maintaining only the slightest of touch until she issues a quite groan and I kiss her for a long moment.

As I position myself above her, pinning her arms to the bed either side of the pillow, using my knees to force her thighs apart, we are ready to become one, but Mai has taught me better than that and instead I probe my shaft across her pubic bone. Within a few strokes she is breathing deeply and issuing tiny groans. A few more and her eyes are closed and she begins to whisper, "Oh, please," and slides her hand down to direct me into her.

As she holds me in her hand I whisper in her ear, "What do you want?"

"Yes, I want it," she gasps.

"What?" I whisper again, hovering millimeters from where she wants me.

"Your cock, your cock inside me," Nancy says quietly.

"My cock inside you," I repeat sliding it through her moistness.

"Just fuck me, oh, just fuck me," she pleads and removes her hand from my shaft and begins to rub herself.

I dip myself into her, feeling her fingers rotating, and then slide back out until I am barely touching her swollen lips, she rubs more vigorously. Nancy groans and I slide slightly forward again, then immediately withdraw so I rest on the soft skin between her openings, sliding up almost to the point of penetration and then down again, slowly, repeatedly. Nancy groans and wraps a leg around my back and claws at my shoulders in an attempt to draw me all the way into her. She pleads again, "Fuck me, just fuck me."

Enjoying her torment, wanting to play the game as superbly as Mai, I move back a little so I can reach an erect nipple with my mouth. As I flick my tongue across her breast I slide my hand down to feel the wetness between her legs and insert two fingers inside her. Gently pushing my fingers deeper my mouth slides along her stomach until her soft pubic hair touches my lips. Gliding my fingers in and out I play my tongue across her little bump, up and down her lips, inside and out. Nancy grasps hold of the back of my head to hold it firmly in place and pushes herself forward so her legs are spread to their maximum arc. A slight quiver runs up the inside of her thigh, she is near to climax, I lift my mouth and fingers out of her, bringing my cock up to touch the swollen petals of her flower, dripping with lubrication and saliva.

Wavering on the precipice, eyes closed, legs spread as far apart as possible, groaning, reaching her arms down trying to get a hold on my hips to draw me in. Nancy squirms and groans beneath me as I slowly dip in and out of her, ever so slightly. "Just fuck me," she pleads as I withdraw once again. "Fuck me," this time it is a demand.

I finally enter her and push, ever so slowly, deeper and deeper, until our hips are joined and I can penetrate no further, yet I keep pushing and grinding, rocking forward and back causing our pelvic bones to grate over the top of each other's until I feel her muscles clench around me as she shudders into the beginnings of an orgasm. I watch her lose control of her expression as her mind is blasted into that otherworldly place of surging endorphins and blinding white light. Her muscles tense, causing her legs to straighten and go rigid, the shuddering increases, she grabs hold of the pillow and clenches her fist until her knuckles turn white. I raise my body up and thrust into her again and again, drawing myself all the way out and then plunging all the way in again, over and over until her face contorts as though she is choking and then it is over and her mind returns, opening her eyes, bathed in a serine post orgasmic glow.

Later, when Nancy is sleeping, it is Carmen where my mind settles as I drift into darkness.

ERECT NIPPLES

Nancy is still sleeping among the junk and I sit smoking on the beer crate out in front of the room enjoying the ducks and swans paddling in the canal. The beach is taking form, I've built the pylons out of paving stones. It was a big effort to drag them down from Pusher Street on the rackety old hand cart, but it was worth it. They now form sturdy foundations a couple of metres out into the water. Today I will lay four big, thick railway sleepers from the canal's bank out onto the pylons to form two large triangles, creating the illusion of land meeting the water. I have also ordered five cubic metres of sand from the Green Hall in Christiania and a truck will dump it at the end of Dussen where Christiania meets the city, not far from where Kalle's house is. I have to wheelbarrow two tonnes of sand about half a kilometre. It will be a slow job and physically straining, but in a way I look forward to it. I always enjoy the ache of muscles following a hard day's work and it will only make a visit to the Bathhouse more enjoyable. I have also built a sturdy rock retaining wall with the paving stones, to create a terrace in Kalle's backyard. All in all I am content with the plan for Kalle's beach and am looking forward to see the finished result.

I don't see him much, but every couple of days Kalle comes down to see how things are going. Generally he has a look of horror on his face when he sees my half-completed work, thinking I don't have a plan and am simply dumping rocks into the canal.

The door to my little room opens up and out steps Nancy wearing nothing but a small pair of cotton briefs, her pert breasts naked in the morning sun, tiny erect nipples poking in my direction. She sits down resting her back against a tree and watches me as I start to heave the huge railway sleepers into position on the stone pylons and then fix some final wooden slats, to hold the sand, onto the bottom. I work through the cool of the mid-morning as Nancy reads one of the books that I have collected in my time at Christiania, a book about Buddhism that old Bill from the Kosmic Bloomst gave to me. Soon my work is complete and Nancy and I walk up through Dussen across the lake and into the centre of Christiania for tea and joints at the Moonfisher. Nancy studies at university and she leaves for classes while I, of course, enjoy the next few hours sweating in the Bathhouse sauna.

ANEKA

It has taken the best part of two and half days to cart the sand down the dirt track through Dussen and onto the beach. Two tonnes of sand didn't sound like much when I ordered it from the Green Hall, but it has taken around fifty wheelbarrow loads to move it all. The residents of Dussen, sitting on their front porches or working in their gardens, laugh as I stagger past with the wheelbarrow, time after time. Kalle comes to check on the beach's progress and he can finally see what I've been trying to achieve. He stands out the back of his house and smiles.

"My daughter will love it," he says and I can sense the tenderness in his heart, this big, macho outlaw biker, melting under the intensity of his emotions for his daughter. "I like it," he tells me and pulls a thick wad of cash from his pocket, counts out a thousand kroner, and hands it to me. "Good job."

The beach is vast, forty feet long and ten feet wide, twenty at the apex of the two triangles that stretches out into the canal. I sit, bare feet squeezing fine sand granules between my toes, and wonder at my accomplishment. I have never built anything before this, besides the stairs at the side of Kalle's house, and have a great sense of achievement. I sit for hours smoking joints and supping Tuborg beer savoring the satisfaction of the results of my hard labor and creativity. It actually feels like a beach, with enough sand to make sandcastles and large enough to be immersed in a true beach experience.

Feeling elated I spend a good few hours in the Bathhouse and then the Moonfisher until late into the eternal Scandinavian dusk. A band plays at the end of Pusher Street near the Woodstock Bar and a small crowd has gathered. Two of the Machine Hall garbage run guys are in the band. Kevin, with his shining bald head and stocky frame, plays a base instrument made out of a broom handle nailed to a big wooden box that amplifies the sound. He holds the single string with his thumb at varying intervals up the length of the broomstick to create different notes as he plays. Jess, another of the Machine Hall guys, the Swiss who pretends to be French, sings: "When there are so many fish in the sea, how come I get those crabs – how come I get those crabs."

The song resonates with me. Since the Italian Angel helped me find my butterfly wings I have been itching quite badly around the groin and fear I too have gotten those crabs.

The crowd is jigging and dancing away, slapping their knees in jest to the hillbilly tunes that the box band plays. Among the crowd I spot Aneka, my fish that got away, Whether it is all the sex that I've had recently or I just don't want to beat a dead horse, I'm not sure, but either way I've finally lost interest in her. When she spots me looking her way I pull a funny face and continue to dance off to the side of the crowd. This time, the only time I don't try with her, she dances up next to me and says, "Hi, hi, want a drink?"

"Vodka!"

"Sure," she says, and smiles as she takes my hand to walk us over to Nemoland. We slam a shot of vodka and take beers to sit by a fire burning in a barrel, the very same fire I stood next to when I arrived in Christiania. It seems so long since I was spit forth from the freeway to Freetown Christiania. I stare into the flames and from deep inside an itch for distance begins to stir.

"Hungry?" Aneka asks after a period of silence. "Follow me." She grabs hold of my hand and takes me to her apartment, a short distance into the city. She cooks a simple meal and I do the dishes, which amazes her. "Danish men never do the dishes!"

Whether it is the dishes I have done or my poetry that I read her, she looks at me in such a way that I know that she is mine. However, as I look at Aneka I can think only of Carmen and wonder where she is. There has been so much sex recently and none of it has included love. The more sex I have the more I seem to realise that Carmen is where love is to be found. The Italian Angel, Mai and Nancy, all coming and going from the little junk-filled room at any hour during the day or night and the more they come the more Carmen seems to occupy my mind. Sex without love has begun to leave an empty, hollow space inside that leaves me hungry for love and thinking of Carmen. And with such thoughts in my mind I say goodnight to Aneka and make my way back through the city to Christiania and my junk-filled room.

THE BATLE OF CHRISTIANIA

Working at the Moonfisher, I chisel out a space in one of the fence posts making it ready to slot in and bolt on a fence paling. "Good job," says Axel, leaning over my shoulder. "Nice and strong, let's see them kick it down now, eh?"

I chisel away, enjoying the sun on my back. It's late morning and there's a crowd in the park drinking tea and smoking joints. Janis Joplin plays softly from the Moonfisher's speakers. I truly love this place, but I can still feel the nagging for distance, for movement. I ponder the feeling, breathing deeply trying to empty my mind and allow my thoughts to truly reveal themselves.

"Police!" comes a shout from the behind the Woodstock Bar, over by Pusher Street.

"Police!" echoes the call from someone in the park and people, all at once, stand up. Dogs start barking and someone's tea is spilt smashing glass out front of the Moonfisher. No one is quite sure what to do until Lunar comes running out of the Moonfisher door. "Run, c'mon," she yells, waving her hands to encourage people to join her at a jog down towards Pusher Street.

"Oh crap," says Axel. "We'll never get this bloody fence finished. Here, give me your chisel." Like any good tradesman his first concern is for the tools. I like Axel, so instead of following my first instinct to run with the crowd, I help him gather up all the tools and lock them away in the shed behind the Moonfisher. Before we have finished, the Moonfisher has lost all of its patrons and is now left a desolate building. Eeveryone has dashed off to Pusher Street to see what is going on. This is strange, as the other day when a couple of old policemen turned up on Pusher Street everyone ran away. Now, everyone is running towards them. With the tools packed away, Axel and I stroll over towards Pusher Street where a large crowd is gathering. More and more people come out of Christiania's various buildings and stream past us heading to Pusher Street. It's difficult to see what is going on as the crowd has become quite large. Beyond the gates of Christiania I can see the flashing lights of police cars swirling their red and blue glow above the heads of the crowd, reflecting off the buildings.

People are talking to one another, asking questions, trying to figure out what the situation is and I'm jostled from behind as the crowd grows larger still. Its momentum carries me down Pusher Street towards the main gate, like a sheep in a herd driven towards the slaughter house.

The crowd is beginning to shout and jeer at the police, who I still can't see. I swim through the crowd to a bench made from thick railway sleepers and stand on it to see the police for the first time. About fifteen of them form their frontline with many more behind, perhaps as many as one hundred. They are in full riot gear, dressed in black with heavy armour: chest guards, thick gloves and helmets with bulbous visors pulled down over their faces. Each of them carries a large clear plastic shield held out in front with one hand, while the other holds a thick black truncheon. All have gas masks strapped to their combat webbing and some carry grenade launchers with large circular magazines. The police frontline advances slowly down Pusher Street towards the crowd. As they shuffle their way forward the crowd inches back, maintaining a wide gap. From the crowd emerges a photographer who bends down onto one knee before the police line and starts snapping shots. He is joined by a second photographer and another. A man with a video camera joins them and soon the entire frontline of the crowd is made up of photographers who shuffle backwards taking photos of the police line.

The police are now well inside Christiania and into a small, wider stretch of Pusher Street known as The Kitchen. The increased space means that the crowd disperses to either side of the police line so that the police become flanked on each side. They keep their rank, but look a little nervous with their flanks occupied. More police are entering Christiania from the city, coming down Pusher Street from the main gates and past the Machine Hall. Nothing's happening though as the front line of the police have stopped their advance now that they are flanked on three sides. Their shields are locked tightly together protecting them like a phalanx of roman soldiers. The photographers stand right up to the faces of the police's front rank taking photos, brazen in getting so close. The police do nothing, seemingly awaiting orders, and the crowd, seeing nothing is about to happen, relaxes. For now the police seem happy to have simply made their entrance into Christiania and down Pusher Street.

Needless to say all the pushers are gone and there is no hash to be seen anywhere. From out of the crowd steps Kalle, I hadn't noticed him until now. He steps away from the crowd towards the police line. In his hand is a giant joint on a long mamut. He puts the joint to his lips and takes a long draw making a show of how much he can suck into his lungs. His chest swells up and he holds his breath, smiles at the policeman standing in front of him, then exhaling a long stream of smoke that hits the policeman's visor and swirls around it. I doubt the smoke reaches the policeman's lungs through his protective equipment, but the gesture isn't wasted on the crowd which cheers. The police do nothing, still waiting for orders. Kalle remains where he stands, three or four paces out from the crowd, alone in no-man's land, and takes another long toke and blows it out across the police line. The photographers are snapping away at Kalle in his defiance from all angles.

Behind the first line of police a search is being conducted. More police in riot gear are turning over tables, looking in bins, searching for any hash that the pushers have left behind. A couple of marijuana plants that have been growing along the sides of Pusher Street are pulled up and shoved into black plastic bags. The crowd jeers and a few people in the frontline step forward, distressed at seeing their beloved plants pulled up. The police react by lifting their truncheons ready to strike, but they don't need to as those who stepped forward from the crowd quickly retreat back. Neither the crowd nor the police seem to want to escalate the situation and for a while a stalemate ensures.

A young girl pushes her way to the front of the crowd and starts handing out small plastic bottles. The crowd unscrews the lids and draw out small loops dripping in a gleaming fluid, then blows a cloud of bubbles out towards the police line. Hundreds, thousands of bubbles float towards the police popping as they hit the riot shields and helmet visors, a wall of bubbles protecting the crowd. The photographers love it, snapping shots of the gleaming spheres as they drift before the perspex of the police shields.

From behind the crowd a snare drum sounds the rasping beat of a military march, rap, rap, rapping away on a cowhide with the distinct sound of a beaded snare. Working a slower beat is the regular boom boom of a base drum. "The Clown Army!" someone in the crowd shouts, "Make way for the Clown Army!"

From my high vantage point I see a line of about twenty clowns, dressed in red with the distinct yellow circles of the Christiania flag painted on their shirts and down the side of their puffy trousers. The first two clowns carry the drums the first the snare, the second a large base drum held by a strap around the clown's neck.

Thrumpety, thrump, thrump, boom, thrumpety thrump, thrump, boom!

The clowns march in a column through the parting crowd towards the police. They wear bright hats and red noses held to their faces with thin chords of elastic. Some have faces painted white, others wear clown masks. Thrumpety, thrump, thrump, boom. "Halt!" yells one of the clowns and they stop. "Form ranks!" The clown sergeant bellows his order in a loud militaristic voice and the clowns form rank in front of the police. The Clown army and the riot police face each other in an eerie silence.

The crowd has pushed back to allow the Clown Army enough space. Some of the clowns have party kazoos, which they blow to unravel their paper length in the direction of the police, a taunting gesture. As the clowns arrive so too have more police reinforcements, including what appears to be their commander. The police commander signals with his arm for the front rank to move forward and, with well rehearsed precision, the frontline of riot police step forward in unison, banging their truncheons against their perspex shields with a deafening crash. Instead of falling back each member of the Clown Army collapses to the ground as though they have been shot. They clutch their stomachs and roll on the ground some stretching their arms out to the crowd in mock pleas of help. They lay sprawled on the street and the riot police are forced to break their composed frontline as they step, and trip, over the line of fallen clowns.

The crowd becomes distressed as the riot police advance beyond the splayed clowns. Some people turn and try to wiggle their way through the crowd away from the police, while others are coming forward. Bubbles continue to float in the breeze. The initial stalemate has ended and a new feeling spreads throughout the crowd. Concern, worry, but not quite yet panic. The front of the crowd which was initially made up of those who arrived first, has now been replaced by hardcore Christianites, mostly young males and middle-aged men. Women are still present, but are at the edges, pushed up along the walls of the buildings that line the north side of Pusher Street. The lighthearted jeers originally aimed at the police have been replaced by angry sneers and vicious gestures of hand and fist. The police continue to push forward, never breaking their line, obviously well trained. From over the back of the crowd flies a tomato that splats across a perspex shield, then comes an egg that shatters and blinds the view of the shield's wielder with sticky yolk. A small group at the front of the crowd leans their collective shoulder into the advancing wall of shields in an attempt to slow the police's advance. The police commander shouts an order and the line of perspex shields breaks temporarily to allow the second row of riot police to thrust arms through the frontline. They grab one of the young men trying to halt their advance and drag him with surprising force through the police line and down onto the ground. Police in the second rank drop their knees into the man's back and roughly twist his arms around to restrain him. Another set of gloved police hands quickly clasp his arms together with a plastic strap and he is roughly dragged through the police ranks and out of sight. The crowd shouts in unison and more young men throw themselves at the police line as all hell breaks loose. The police line disintegrates as the crowd rushes forward in an attempt to save their comrade. I can see distinct worry behind the bulbous visors of the police. While they have plenty of riot police here the crowd is large and the mood has quickly turned from defiant joviality to blatant anger. Behind the crowd's front line a chant starts. A single voice at first, but quickly a roaring chorus: "Fuck the police! Fuck the police!"

The police are dragging more and more people to the ground, slamming their faces into the paving stones and dropping their full weight onto their knees, thrust into the backs of struggling young men. Other police face the crowd with their shields out and truncheons held high offering protection to those who are tying struggling hands and feet. The police are ready to fight, light on their toes with adrenalin coursing through their veins, their eyes darting back and forth, alert for danger. As people approach in attempts to save their friends, police truncheons are lifted high ready to swing down. Still the photographers circle the police getting right in close to photograph the bloodied faces of those being arrested. Once people are bound with plastic ties, arms locked behind their backs, they are roughly lifted by their elbows by policemen on each arm and one more carrying their legs so the bound protesters are horizontal and facing the ground. On more than one occasion they are dropped, by accident, to smash face first to the ground before being roughly lifted again and carried off to the rear of the police ranks.

The scene has quickly turned very violent and I remain perched on top of the bench on the south side of Pusher Street. When the police look at me I remain motionless and their attention quickly moves to someone in the crowd who is actually a threat to them. I can see the blood lust in the eyes of each policeman that looks my way. They catch my gaze, with shield out and truncheon raised and quickly run a threat assessment on me. I can see they are scared, but also loving the action.

From the flanks of the police a garbage bin of water is thrown and splashes over two of the police instantly soaking them. It is enough to distract their attention, only for a moment, but enough time for a small group of protesters to smash into their bodies and send them sprawling back. With a break in the police line some in the crowd dash forward and attempt to grab one of their own whose feet are in the process of being cuffed. The police won't let go and a brief tug of war begins with the man, hands cuffed behind his back, as the rope. A baton swings down across the forearms of the pulling protestors and the cuffed man is dragged, face bouncing along the paving stones, back behind the police line.

By now half a dozen protestors have been cuffed and I can see them being carried face down towards the front gate of Christiania and the waiting vans. The police are winning, it is obvious, their numbers, armour and training proving too much for the unorganised crowd. The crowd is no longer attacking the front line of police and is quickly dispersing back down Pusher Street towards Grøntsagen. The photographers, somehow protected by the cameras held out before them, remain all around the police who appear to be unfazed by their presence. With the crowd gone the police break ranks and take stock of the situation. They mill around checking on each other's equipment displaying a bond of camaraderie forged through battle.

A black cloud of smoke rises from the gates of Christiania where the police cars and vans are parked with their blue and red lights still swirling. One of the police cars is burning and the black smoke increases as flames lick higher and higher into the air. A group of protesters come sprinting back into Christiania followed by a squad of riot police. A small group of police standing in Pusher Street turn and run towards them. With police in front and behind them, the arsonists are running hard like scared rabbits trying to sidestep the outstretched arms of the oncoming police.

One loses his balance and falls just as a policeman grabs hold of his shirt and he swings around, centrifugal forces carrying his legs out wide. He crashes to the ground and two of the police thrust their knees into his shoulder blades so roughly that I can see the agony shoot across his face. Another of the protesters skirts past the police and is off down Pusher Street literally running for his life. A group of police break after him, but they are slowed by their body armour and he escapes.

A stone, one that didn't make it onto Kalle's beach, flies through the air from the top of Pusher Street and smashes into the helmet of one of the police. He stumbles almost losing his balance before raising his truncheon, charging towards the stone throwing group. He is joined by half a dozen others who have lost all discipline and are now gunning for blood.

"They should just throw eggs," says an old lady standing near me. It's as though she is watching it all happen on TV and not actually standing in the middle of the melee.

"No, they come in with violence and we need to give them the same back," I hear her friend say.

"But we don't want violence like this," says the first lady.

"Violence, they brought the violence. What are we supposed to do?" says the second and they start to bicker with each other on the merits of violence as it erupts all around them.

Up until now the police have shown discipline and acted professionally. Now they are angry. The burning car and the stones hurtling through the air have changed the game and the police are simply looking for anyone to extract revenge from. An old man from Christiania is in among them trying to promote calm by attempting to reason with the police. He's not antagonising them at all, but he is getting in their way and visibly annoying them as they try to determine where the rocks are coming from. Frustrated that more stones are being thrown at them the police reach out and grab the old man and thrust him face first into the ground, splitting the skin above his eye and drawing blood. Despite his age and frailty heavy police knees are thrust into his back and his arms are twisted and lifted up behind him. He howls in pain and the people of Christiania hear. Seemingly from nowhere the crowd returns and attempts to shove the police off the old man. Truncheons are swung connecting with sickening cracks and thuds, and the crowd's rage grows larger still. The police finally realise that things have gotten way out of control. They fall back before the growing crowd that is becoming increasingly angry and brazen in their advance. The police commanders signal a retreat. From my vantage point I can see the police training in action as it restores a semblance of order to the chaos. Their ranks reform into a crooked line, shields locked together protecting them from the barrage of flying objects, both stones and vegetables. They shuffle backwards keeping their shields facing the crowd in a protective wall. As they back step down Pusher Street, past the Machine Hall and closer to Christiania's entrance the crowd stops following them and lets them go. The hail of missiles peters out and eventually stops. The battle is over and the police have lost. A lone Christianite follows them. He wears bright red pants held up with suspenders and he pushes a broom in the direction of the retreating police, sweeping out the garbage, cleaning the streets of Christiania.

CARMEN

Upstairs, Kalle is having a party. I can hear music and the heavy footfalls of the Hell's Angels through the thin floorboards above me as I lay on my bed in Kalle's junk room. I feel numb, the adrenalin from the riot long gone, all I can do is stare at a World War II Nazi infantry helmet that rests in the corner covered in dust with Fuck the Police written across it in white paint.

"Hey, you down there?" I hear Kalle yelling through the floorboards from directly above and he stamps his feet loudly as though he is knocking on a door. "Hey, you down there, Casanova," is what he calls me these days since he has noticed Nancy, Mai and the Italian Angel coming and going from my little junk room. "Come up!"

I'm feeling heavy in both body and mind and lift myself up on an elbow, considering if I am in the mood to party or not. I'm not convinced that I am as I can't shake the desire for Carmen that has wrapped itself around me recently, a dreadful notion that I might have lost this beautiful woman. With Carmen in my thoughts I push my feet into a worn pair of army boots that I wear with the high ankles folded down and stumble up the stairs that I built at the side of Kalle's house, past a couple of huge biker guys, without their Hell's Angels patches, and through the front door. When Kalle sees me he grins. "Hey man, you saw what Christiania can do today? Were you there?"

"Yeah, I was there," I say. "Pretty scary."

"Scary? Fuck, for the police it was, eh? Fuck the police, those pussies! Grab yourself a beer from the fridge."

I sit at the end of his kitchen table and survey the people who are partying in his house. They are mainly big, tattooed guys who I am sure are all Hell's Angels, but they are all unmarked, still scared of Christiania's mothers despite having won a street battle against the riot police. They don't pay me any attention for in their eyes I am just a boy, a skinny one at that, and among these gorillas I'm a nonentity, insignificant. I drink and feel the warmth of the alcohol seep into my bloodstream and through my muscles. Across the room Kalle is rolling a massive joint. When he's done and it's alight I get up and walk over to him, motioning with my hand that I want a toke.

"Oh, careful," he says. "This one is for the lions, not pussycats, very strong." And he coughs and splutters after taking the first toke.

"Just give it to me," I say, a little offended that he thinks me to be a pussycat.

He shrugs and hands it across. It's long, at least twenty centimetres including the ivory mamut, and about two centimetres in diameter at the trumpeted end. I toke on it, taking a long draw while looking Kalle in the eyes attempting to prove that I am, in fact, a lion. I don't cough, but splutter, and blow out a long jet of smoke that wafts up and covers the underside of the ceiling.

"Wow, that is strong." My head is spinning. After a few moments I regain my composure and issue a fake roar, like a lion, at Kalle. He laughs and I ask him, "Why did the police come today?"

"The police, it's their job man, they always come. Every couple of years they send in the riot squad to try to close Christiania down, mainly trying to get rid of Pusher Street really. Society doesn't like us. Some people support us, but most people out there in the straight world hate us. Every few years a new politician gets into power and a new campaign to get rid of Christiania begins and they send in the riot police. I couldn't count how many times it has happened. I know for sure though that it will keep happening. We won today so it will be a while before they try again, but they will. What they don't seem to realise though is that the more they try to get rid of us the more it unites us. You know, I really don't like those guys living in the Gay House or the bloody hippies over at the Blue Caramel. I know that they don't like me either, but when the police come, man, they are my brothers and I fight for them and they fight for me. It is the fact that we have to fight for our survival that makes Christiania so strong. You know what I mean?"

"Yeah, I guess I do, it's kind of special that way. I can feel the strength in Christiania. Not just the kind of strength that kicks the police out, but strength in life, in living. Like most of that straight world shit that gets in my head and controls my thinking doesn't really reach me Christiania."

"What are you talking about?" laughs Kalle. "I have no idea of the straight world, they're all fucking lunatics out there as far as I'm concerned, living the fucking rat race. I can't understand it. I came to Christiania when I was twelve, straight off of the streets. I was never a part of all that straight world shit."

"That's what I mean," I say. "I ran away from that stuff, except I had nowhere like Christiania to go, all I could do was hit the freeways and just go. And I've been going for over two years now, governed by the fate of my thumb hitching those freeways. Everywhere I've ended up has been more or less the same. People worrying about what job they have and what kind of car they drive or house they live in or shirt they fucking wear."

"Yep," says Kalle, nodding. "That's sounds like the straight world."

"But here, in Christiania, none of that stuff matters. It is another world entirely. As soon as I stepped into Christiania I felt all of that stuff just melt away, like it belonged in some other dimension, in some other universe."

"You sound like you're stoned," laughs Kalle.

I am. "You know what though, it's time for me to leave."

"But you've just been telling me how much you love Christiania?" Kalle is perplexed.

"Yeah, I do, but there's a girl."

"Ha, there's always a girl, and plenty more too," says Kalle.

"No, this girl, Carmen, I love her. I think I always have, but I wouldn't allow myself to recognise it before. I guess I didn't want to be tied down, but now I've got to go find her before I lose her to someone else."

"Well," says Kalle. "Know that you are always welcome back here." He passes me the joint again.

Following another toke I begin to feel more the pussycat than the lion and, needing fresh air, walk out of Kalle's front door to stand on his porch. Shouts and calls from the party reach out into the night, echoing across the still, mirror-smooth lake. A tingling feeling streams beneath my skin and fuels a growing urge to get moving again, to get back on the road, score a fix of distance, and find Carmen, wherever she is. Within minutes my bag is packed and slung across my shoulder and, despite the late hour, I walk out through Christiania, out through Copenhagen, to a truck stop at the start of a freeway and go to sleep under an unhitched truck trailer, wondering, where in the world is my love.

SUNRISE RED OVER DENMARK

Sunrise red over Denmark
A fitting morn to my dream
Cold and chilly as the night before
The trucks roaring past they scream:

"Courage and passion
Don't give up young soul
Truth's path leads on to freedom's goal"

I move on in search of dreams
Past windmills and flowers
Wide flats grassed green
Through rolling hills of fertile land
Thumb thrust forth from journeyed hand
From road to car
Then back to road
Day into night
By the freeman's code

As day finds night in blue cloud sky
Truth shines through realities lie
With school dismissed
A man walks free
Sunshine abounds
In a soft cool breeze

EPILOGUE

The events in this book occurred in the early-to-mid nineties. Exacts dates are uncertain as the author wasn't exactly concerned with calendars at the time. Since this time there have been many changes to Christiania, unfortunately mostly for the worse.

In 2001 a centre-right Danish government was elected that promised to end illegal activities within Christiania, and in 2002 it started a campaign to make Christiania's hash trade less visible. In a typically humorous response Christiania covered the stalls on Pusher Street with military camouflage netting. Not amused, the Danish government initiated a huge police operation to once and for all bring an end to the hash trade on Pusher Street. The night before the planned police raid the pushers decided to dismantle their stalls on Pusher Street in order to avoid the inevitable violence such a raid would bring. As a result of the dismantling of Pusher Street the hash trade was pushed underground, with the new distribution networks stretching out into the suburbs of Copenhagen. With the hash trade no longer under the protection of the Christiania community it quickly became influenced by heavily-armed biker and immigrant gangs.

As a sign of the changes, the rules that existed within Christiania during the mid 90's - no violence, no cars, no hard drugs, no biker colors and no selling of homes - has been expanded to include no guns and no bulletproof vests. Sadly they are not always followed. In 2005 a group of masked men burst onto Pusher Street with automatic weapons and gunned down three people, killing one. It is reported that the shootings were conducted by an immigrant gang from Copenhagen who had been attempting to move into Christiania's now underground hash trade (reportedly worth in excess of US$175 million per annum). Four years later, in 2009, a grenade attack occurred at Nemoland within Christiania injuring three people. Thankfully no one was killed this time.

The police have kept up a strong presence within Christiania and the Moonfisher café installed a tally board to count the number of police patrols. From November 2005 to the middle of 2006 over 1000 police patrols occurred within Christiania. This equated to almost six each day consisting of up to 20 police officers dressed in full riot uniform. The Moonfisher now boasts that it is the safest coffee shop in the world.

The author found Carmen and married her, they have three children.

ABOUT THE AUTHOR

Eugine Losse lives in Australia with his wife, Carmen, three children, two dogs, two cats and a cage full of chickens. Having lived within Freetown Christiania's anarchy, Eugines found it difficult to accept authority and was booted from every company that ever employed him. The only choice left was to start his own consulting business and-compete with those who fired him. After a few years Eugine sold his multi-million dollar business as he was detirmined to write this book and spend more time with his young children.

This is Eugine's first book, however, he does have more in him that are beginning to murmer their desire to get out onto the page. Prior to living in Freetown Christiania, Eugine was hitch hiking through the Middle East and, through a chance encounter, found himself living in a Kibutz in the north of Israel. Whether this book about life living in a Marxist community ever sees light of day probably depends on the success of *Freetown Christiania*. If you, the reader, would like to read about Eugine's experiences under communism make sure to let him know via his Facebook page.

Connect with Eugine Losse Online

http://www.facebook.com/profile.php?id=100002994720118
http://www.facebook.com/pages/Freetown-Christiania/209070809158569

Twitter: http://twitter.com/@EugineLosse

mailto:eugine.losse@gmail.com

Like the font cover of this book? Purchase a Banksy the Clown Anarchy T-Shirt at: http://www.printfection.com/counter-culture